Voluntary Sector and Rural Development

Voluntary Sector and Rural Development

Concept, Practice and a New Approach to Remove Rural Poverty

RAJEEB MISRA

RAWAT PUBLICATIONS

Jaipur • New Delhi • Bangalore • Mumbai • Hyderabad • Guwahati

ISBN 81-316-0122-6

Published by
Prem Rawat for **Rawat Publications**
Satyam Apts, Sector 3, Jawahar Nagar, Jaipur 302 004 (India)
Phone: 0141 265 1748 / 7006 Fax: 0141 265 1748
E-mail: info@rawatbooks.com
Website: www.rawatbooks.com

New Delhi Office
4858/24, Ansari Road, Daryaganj, New Delhi 110 002
Phone: 011 2326 3290

Also at Bangalore, Mumbai, Hyderabad and Guwahati

Typeset by Rawat Computers, Jaipur
Printed at Nice Printing Press, New Delhi

Contents

Preface

Since time immemorial, voluntarism has been existing in India by which publicly motivated individuals extend services to the needy in the society. But what distinguishes the current form of voluntarism from its past variant is its institutionalisation and function.

Contribution of Christianity to institutionalisation of charity (a form of voluntarism) worldwide is commendable and well-documented. Since the 19th century A.D. voluntary institutions have come up in India, established by Christian missionaries as well as enlightened Indians. Functions of voluntarism have greatly expanded since 1940s. The new additions are: relief, welfare, development, empowerment, conscientisation, advocacy, sustainable development et al. One of the best known sayings propagated by Ritchie Caider that ushered in the era of development projects for NGOs was that "**give a man a fish and you feed him for today – teach him how to fish and he feeds himself and his family for the rest of their lives.**" Such messages from voluntary sector visionaries have comprehensively changed the functional domain of voluntarism after the World War II. It has grown very vast and has acquired the title of third sector of the society, the first two being State and

Business sectors. The organisations channelling the voluntarism are known as Non-Governmental Organisations or NGOs.

In the modern times, one of the leading functions of these organisations has been rural development and uplift of the poor. NGOs have entered this difficult area due to lack of success on the part of the government or other agencies of the State to bring about any significant change for the better in socio-economic conditions of the people. After the NGO explosion of 1980s and 1990s there has come into existence hundreds and thousands of such agencies all over the country, so much so that the Government of India has drawn up a plan for partnership with NGOs in recognition of the merits of the sector.

I first planned to study this phenomenon sometime back in 1990 noticing their unusually fast growth. In 1993 while applying for registration for Ph.D. at Utkal University, I gave it as topic. On getting permission of the University to pursue the research, I have taken six long years to collect sufficient relevant material to analyse the subject matter, based thereupon conduct the field study, and complete the thesis. I have tried to be as much informative as possible in analysing the theoretical basis of NGOs. This is due to my belief that **theory sustains practice and a good theory supports a good practice.**

The present work is an adaptation of the thesis, entitled *Non-Governmental Organisations in Rural Development: A Case Study of Puri District in Orissa*, in a proper readable form, catering to all classes of readers having interest in the subject. I would recommend the readers to refer to the original thesis submitted to the University in case of any need for further details or doubt about the *modus operandi* of the study and the manner of arriving at conclusions from the study. As such the essential details of a thesis based on empirical study do not form part of the framework of this work to help the reader escape the avoidable monotony of going through a rigorous process of data analysis.

I am sure this book will be found useful by students, theorists, practitioners of voluntarism, and those engaged in tying up of partnerships with this sector including officials in governments.

Rajeeb Misra

Acknowledgements

I wish to record my gratitude to Dr. Amareswar Mishra, Professor of Political Science, Utkal University, Vani Vihar, Bhubaneswar for having given me the opportunity to work as a scholar under his supervision and guidance. I convey my gratefulness to him for sparing his valuable time to my frequent calls in person and over phone clarifying the doubts I had during the course of research.

I am thankful to my wife, Aloka, for extending help in typing the drafts where required, preparing the programmes for data feeding, and the actual act of feeding the data into the laptop, and preparing a number of diagrams (for the thesis that was the precursor of the present book) in an attractive way. I am grateful to the support she provided in the family, shouldering most of the responsibilities during the course of preparation of the thesis as well as this book. I am also thankful for her moral support throughout the course of the study, without which the project could not have been completed.

I am obliged to the following individuals, institutes, libraries, organisations and offices for providing me the facility of library in connection with this research work and/or discussing with me for my further enlightenment in the matter: National Institute of Rural Development, Hyderabad; British Council Library, Mumbai; Indira Gandhi Institute of

Management Studies, Mumbai; Tata Institute of Social Sciences, Mumbai; Bankers Institute of Rural Development, Lucknow and its chief librarian, **Mr. Y Devaramani,** for his personal interest in providing me the required books and periodicals; the library of National Bank Staff College, Lucknow; Centre of Youth and Social Development, Bhubaneswar and **Mr. Jagadananda**, its General Secretary; NISWAS, Bhubaneswar; Xavier Institute of Management Bhubaneswar; CARE, Bhubaneswar; **Mr. Amulya Kumar Mohanty**, Technical Support Coordinator, CASHE Project, CARE; Action Aid; Indian Institute of Public Administration, New Delhi, Social Science Documentation Centre, Indian Council of Social Science Research, New Delhi; National Library, Calcutta; Parija Library, Utkal University; Orissa University of Agriculture and Technology, Bhubaneswar; Orissa State Archives; State Library, Bhubaneswar; Gopabandhu Academy of Administration, Bhubaneswar; Bureau of Statistics and Economics, Bhubaneswar; DRDA, Puri; DDM, NABARD, Puri; BDO, Sadar Block.

I thank Mr. A.B. Mishra, former Professor IGNOU, Bhubaneswar for sparing his time and giving me useful tips on the topic of research, and my brother Mr. Sanjeeb Mishra, who assisted me with all back-up support like draft typing, copying, and coordinating on this work.

Finally, I thank NABARD, particularly Dr. K.G. Karmakar, MD, for granting me permission to pursue the research **during his tenure as CGM of Orissa R.O.**

While the credit for all this must go to the above-mentioned persons, institutes, officials, etc., I stand responsible for the shortcomings and lapses that the work might have contained.

This book that has been developed from the thesis I submitted to Utkal University is dedicated to my **father** who was as much concerned for its completion as I was, and to my late **father-in-law** who loved knowledge and learning.

List of Abbreviations

ANGO	Advocacy NGO
BDO	Block Development Officer
CARE	Co-operative for American Relief Everywhere
CB	Commercial Bank
CYSD	Centre for Youth and Social Development
DCCB	District Central Co-operative Bank
DRDA	District Rural Development Agency
DWACRA	Development of Women and Children in Rural Areas
ESCAP	Economic and Social Commission for Asia and the Pacific
FAO	Food and Agriculture Organization
FCRA	Foreign Contributions Regulation Act
GNP	Gross National Product
GONGO	Governmental Non-Governmental Organisations
GP	Gram Panchayat
GRO	Grassroots Organisation
GRSO	Grassroots Support Organisation

IRDP	Integrated Rural Development Programme
IRMA	Institute of Rural Management Anand
LDA	Local Development Association
LIC	Life Insurance Corporation of India
NABARD	National Bank for Agriculture and Rural Development
NCDP	National Community Development Programme
NDNGO	Non-Developmental NGO
NGDO	Non-Governmental Development Organisation
NGO	Non-Governmental Organisation
ONGO	Operational NGO
PO	People's Organisation
PS	Panchayat Samiti
PSC	Public Service Contractor
PVO	Private Voluntary Organisation
SC	Scheduled Caste
SHG	Self-Help Group
SSI	Small Scale Industry
ST	Scheduled Tribe
TRYSEM	Training of Rural Youth for Self-Employment
VA	Voluntary Agency
VO	Voluntary Organisation
XIMB	Xavier Institute of Management, Bhubaneswar

Introduction

Without a doubt, the past twenty years has produced more social entrepreneurs than terrorists.

– ***David Bornstein***

> Voluntary organisations play a vital role in shaping and implementation of participatory democracy.... They have been contributing immensely...towards various development programmes. They work at grassroots level even in remote areas and...their reach is much wider. They are closer to ground realities and know the needs of the communities. Their approach with target groups is direct, emphatic and...they are able to draw more contextualised plans of action. They also manage to develop intimate contacts with people and develop confidence among them.[1]

The above lines, though appear like comments from NGO quarters or their sympathisers, do in reality constitute the opening remarks of the *Report of the Steering Committee on Voluntary Sector for the Tenth Five-Year Plan (2002-07)* of the Planning Commission, Government of India.

Five decades after government's planned effort in rural development and poverty eradication, there are still a whopping

1. *Report of the Steering Committee on Voluntary Sector for the Tenth Five-Year Plan (2002-07)*, Planning Commission, Government of India, p.1.

25 per cent of the total population below the official poverty line.[2] Out of 192 (138)[3] million households in India, 32 (27) million have no drinking water facility in their premises, 83 (77) million have no electricity or use kerosene for lighting purpose, 122 (108) million have no toilets even of rudimentary type, 103 (91) million have no drainage (even open drainage) for waste water disposal, 68 (55) million have no kitchens in their houses or cook in the open, 124 (97) million are unable to access banking facilities in view of utter poverty, 132 (112) million have no TVs at home, 175 (133) million have no telephones, and 109 (79) million do not even have bicycles for communication.[4] The failures of the government are too obvious. This has indeed prompted it to look for modifications in the existing approaches to rural development or explore alternative approaches. The realisation of the government came sometime around the Seventh Five-Year Plan (1985-90), and, accordingly, emphasis was given to partnership with NGOs in consideration of their foregoing virtues.[5]

---

2. www.indexmundi.com/g/g.aspx?c=in&v=69 quoted from *CIA World Factbook.*
3. The figures in brackets relate to rural areas.
4. Source: www.census.org.
5. During the **Fourth** and **Fifth Plan** periods, the thrust on public cooperation and involvement of people's organisation was lost due to attack on territory and recession that followed. During this period investment was focussed especially in intensive agricultural programmes. In the **Sixth Five-Year Plan**, the idea of participation of people's organisations was again recognised.... Role of VOs in development got a further fillip in the **Seventh Five-Year Plan** where it was declared that serious efforts would be made to involve VOs in various development programmes to supplement the government efforts to offer the rural poor choices and alternatives. See *Report of the Steering Committee on Voluntary Sector for the Tenth Five-Year Plan (2002-07)*, Planning Commission, Government of India, pp.7-8.

It goes to the credit of the voluntary sector that the government today recognises the good work done by the NGOs and has come to a stage seeking cooperation with NGOs. This has come through a historical process which can be traced to 1970s when hundreds of restless citizens in India came out of their confinement to offer voluntary work with a view to resolving the problems of rural development.[6] In the mid-1980s many professionals joined voluntary service with the same objective.[7] With the increase in international aid for NGO activities, the country went through NGO booms in 1980s and 1990s. The government slowly but more and more realised the potentials of the voluntary sector, and consequently, moved in the direction of partnership with NGOs of proven track record. To ensure that the full potential contribution of voluntary organisations is realised, the Planning Commission advised that "the fullest possible communication and cooperation between national, state and local governments and NGOs should be promoted in institutions mandated and programmes designed to carry out various schemes."[8]

The trend around the world is no different. All over the world, the fastest-growing segment of the society is the nonprofit sector, as millions of ordinary people – social entrepreneurs – are increasingly stepping in to solve problems where governments and bureaucracies have failed. **Without a doubt,**

---

6. Kapoor, A.K. and Singh, Dharamvir, *Rural Development through NGOs*, Rawat Publications, 1997, pp. 20-21.

   Also see Riddel, Roger and Robinson, Mark, *Non-Governmental Organizations and Rural Poverty Alleviation,* Overseas Development Institute, London, Clarendon Press, Oxford, 1995, p. 141.

7. *Ibid.*

8. *Report of the Steering Committee on Voluntary Sector for the Tenth Five-Year Plan (2002-07)*, Planning Commission, Government of India, p.1.

the past twenty years has produced more social entrepreneurs than terrorists.[9] The observation speaks of the shape that the voluntary movement has taken, most of which have gone unreported in the world media. In recognition of the role of voluntarism, the UN General Assembly in its 52nd session declared the year 2001 as the International Year of Volunteers.[10]

The role of NGOs was particularly recognised at the United Nations Conference on Environment and Development held in Rio de Janeiro in June 1992. Thereafter, active presence of NGOs continued at all important global international forums, such as the Cairo Population Conference 1994, the Copenhagen World Summit on Social Development 1995 and the Beijing Conference on Women 1995.

Today, NGOs are serving millions of citizens in scores of countries. Their reach and scope often eclipse both the private and public sector, touching and affecting the lives of every citizen, often more profoundly than the forces of the market place or the agencies and bureaucracies of government.[11] In India today, there are more than 50,000 active development oriented NGOs, of which not less than 13,000 NGOs have availed assistance from the Government of India alone on

---

9. See for details Bornstein, David, *How to Change the World: Social Entrepreneurs and the Power of New Ideas,* Oxford University Press, 2003.
10. In November 1997, the United Nations General Assembly proclaimed 2001 as the International Year of Volunteers (IYV). Main objectives of the Year were increased recognition, facilitation, networking and promotion of volunteering.
    See www.worldvolunteerweb.org/events/iyv/
11. Fisher, Julie, *Nongovernments: Political Development of the Third World*, Kumarian Press, 1998 (see Foreword by Jeremy Rifkin, p. vii).

different projects and programmes.[12] With the call of the government to deepen further the government-NGO cooperation, the role of NGOs is bound to increase manifolds. In the context of increasing responsibility for NGOs and trust reposed in them by funders, it has become all the more necessary now to understand the nature and role these new institutions are playing and are capable of, especially, in an area such as rural development which is full of pitfalls.

In this background, an effort has been made to deal with NGO conceptually and analyse its growth, structure, function and relationship in all its manifestations. The theoretical handling of the topic is bound to help us understand the innermost aspects of NGO that lead to better transactions with and within the institution in question in field conditions. Further, in keeping with the theme of the book, a conceptual treatment of terms such as *development* and *rural development* has been undertaken and the history of rural development in India, from the ancient age to the modern times, has been traced to enable the reader to better appreciate the subject in the present context. A space has also been devoted to a brief description of the objectives behind each of the important initiatives and programmes of rural development implemented during five-year plans starting from the first to the tenth. An annexure to the present text gives details of the programmes for voluntary sector implemented through ministries/departments of the Government of India, which can be of much help to students and practitioners of voluntarism in deciding the nature of collaboration they can seek *vis-à-vis* government.

---

12. See Nanavathy, Meher and Kulkarni, P.D., *NGOs in the Changing Scenario*, Uppal Publishing House, 1998, p.3.

    Report of the Steering Committee on Voluntary Sector for the Tenth Five-Year Plan (2002-07), Planning Commission, Government of India, p.10.

After dealing with the theory of NGO and rural development, there follows a picture of the real world of Indian NGOs through a micro study conducted in Puri district of the state of Orissa. The findings are neither in all praise of NGOs nor do they take away fully the credit of NGOs that this sector has so far acquired for itself. They are important from the point of view that there are elements in the study which can help the voluntary sector in taking stock of its strong as well as weak points and thereupon working to refashion NGOs in service for the better. Nevertheless, the voluntary sector being largely without checks and control until now, the ultimate balance sheet of its success and failure *vis-à-vis* its constituents' vision and mission would lie in the age-old Indian saying as contained in the Mundaka Upanishad – *Satymeva Jayate* (truth alone triumphs).

1

NGOs: Concept

Voluntarism is as pervasive and permanent as individualism or bureaucracy. The degree of purity of voluntary work reflects the degree of purity of the civic life of a people.

– ***Author's reflection***

Why NGOs

The civil society is playing an increasingly important social and economic role around the world. One of the more positive moves of the 1980s has been recognition of the essential development role of civil society. People are creating new institutions at both the local and national levels to provide for needs that are not being met by either the market place or the public sector.[1]

According to Jeremy Rifkin, the society is "a three-legged stool made up of the market sector, government sector, and civil sector. The first leg creates **market capital**, the second leg creates **public capital**, and the third leg creates **social capital**.... Finding a balance between the market, government and civil sectors becomes paramount...."[2] The civil sector "consists of the

1. Korten, David C., *Getting to the 21st Century: Voluntary Action and the Global Agenda*, Kumarian Press, 1990, p.95.
2. Fisher, Julie, *Nongovernments: Political Development of the Third World*, Kumarian Press, 1998 (See Foreword by Jeremy Rifkin, p.vii).

millions of citizens who give of their time each week serving in the many NGOs that make up the sprawling civil society."[3] Such organisations, basically charities, grew up following the World War II. They are today called **Non-Governmental Organisations (NGOs)** in Europe and **Private Voluntary Organisations (PVOs)** in North America.[4]

The widespread belief that development is primarily a task of the government has legitimated authoritarianism and created a major barrier to true development in the South. The people have been expected to put their faith and resources in the hands of government, and in return governments have promised to bring about development. This promise has proved to be false, and it was based on an over-assessment of the capacity of government and of the nature of development itself.[5] In this background, "many NGOs became increasingly aware during the 1980s that the leadership needed to deal with the underlying causes of the human tragedy was not being provided by governments. Governments and international agencies themselves came to acknowledge the ability of NGOs to do what many governments have proven unable to do, i.e., to get a range of essential goods and services to the poor."[6] NGOs now have greater diversity, credibility and creativity than ever before. In the developing countries they have often managed to engage

---

3. *Ibid.*, p.viii.
4. Poulton, Robin and Harris, Michael (Eds.), *"On Charities and NGOs, by Michael Harris," Putting People First: Voluntary Organisations and Third World Development*, Macmillan, 1988, p.1.

   The author adds: In many ways it is a pity that the word 'charity' has been displaced, as it is a constant reminder that compassion must always have its place in NGO activities. *Ibid.*
5. Korten, David C., *op. cit.,* 1990, p.95.
6. *Ibid.*, p.5.

with local populations and to command their trust in ways which governments find impossible.[7]

It is said that organisations get created because that seems like the most natural way of functioning. Two main reasons for creating NGOs are rooted in two different priorities. The first one relates to providing a collective mechanism to pursue the commitment to work. This mechanism becomes the organisation. The other route for creating an organisation is based on the requirements of projects. Increasingly project funds are available only to organised initiatives, and not to individuals. Many non-government voluntary development organisations have come about because of this requirement.[8]

Understanding NGOs

The Concise Oxford Dictionary of Current English defines **non-government** as **"not belonging to or associated with a**

---

7. Clark, John, *Democratizing Development: The Role of Voluntary Organizations*, Kumarian Press, 1991, p.3.

   Clark further says: The enhanced role of NGOs comes at a time when the thinking of the more established actors – the official development agencies – is in considerable disarray. Development, as they define it, isn't working. *Ibid.*

8. *Voluntary Development Organizations in India: A Study of History, Roles and Future Challenges*, Society for Participatory Research in Asia, New Delhi, November 1991, p.67.

   It is when individual pursuit of such a commitment becomes difficult that a collective mechanism needs to be created. *Ibid.*

   "Much of today's international development effort is directed at a variety of organizations and institutions – social change is seldom achieved by an individual acting alone." See Fowler, Alan, *Striking a Balance: A Guide to Enhancing the Effectiveness of Non-Governmental Organisations in International Development*, Earthscan Publications Ltd., London, 1997, p.20.

government."[9] According to David Korten, "**any organization that is both non-governmental and nonprofit is generally considered to be an NGO**". This includes a bewildering variety of organisations that have little in common with one another."[10]

The World Bank's working definition is inclusive, specifying only that such organisations be: (a) largely or entirely independent of governments; (b) working for humanitarian or co-operative rather than commercial ends, and to relieve suffering, promote the interests of the poor, protect the environment, provide basic social services, or undertake community development.[11]

The term NGO, though a negative formation, tends to incorporate a wide range of development promoting voluntary organisations. Thus NGO seems to be a category of development promoting organisations which are initiatives voluntarily taken by citizens, professionals, youngsters to focus their attention on one of the developmental aspects of their specific context.[12]

Often the term NGDO – **Non-Governmental Development Organisation** – is used in the literature concerning NGOs. According to Michael Edwards and Alan Fowler, NGDOs are intermediaries working primarily on issues of poverty and injustice within developing countries and at global level, and they form the majority of the groups that have grown

9. *The Concise Oxford Dictionary of Current English,* Ninth Edition, Oxford University Press, 1995, p.926.

10. Korten, David C., *op. cit.*, p.95.

11. *World Bank Operational Directives,* 14.70, The World Bank, Washington D.C., 1989, p.1.

12. Tandon, Rajesh, *NGO-Government Relations: A Source of Life or a Kiss of Death*, Society for Participatory Research in Asia, New Delhi, p.3.

dramatically over the last ten years. Thus, **NGDOs are a subset of NGOs.**[13]

A report prepared by the Institute of Rural Management, Anand, India describes NGDOs as those organisations that respond exclusively to a social need for providing development services to disadvantaged people and operate as nonprofit human service organisations. NGDOs are created as non-government agencies to provide to their beneficiaries specific services not otherwise available from the market. They cater to a specific target group and resource dependent on private patrons and state, etc. Their output is hard to measure because of the nature of their services. Their motivation for work is different from that of profit seeking ones. They provide a set of services, which are not governed by market forces, and offer their services only to people who cannot pay for them. The resource providers and service recipients of NGDOs are distinct and different.[14]

Position of NGOs in Society

Norman Uphoff, in his work, *Why NGOs are not a Third Sector* argues a case for three areas of decision-making and action corresponding to the **public sector**, the **private sector** and a very different third sector. This third sector, according to him, can be

13. For details see Edwards, Michael and Fowler Alan, (Eds.), *Introduction: Changing Challenges for NGDO Management* by Michael Edwards and Alan Fowler, *The Earthscan Reader on NGO Management*, Earthscan, 2003, p.2.

    This may stand in contrast to Rajesh Tandon's view that NGOs are development promoting organisations, implying that NGOs and NGDOs are not different (this is author's own assessment).

14. *IRMA MDO* Workshop Report: *Workshop of Research Partners in a Nationwide Collaborative Research Programme Inquiring into Management of Development Organizations,* Institute of Rural Management Anand, May 1994, pp. 20-21.

referred to as the **membership sector,**[15] the voluntary sector or the collective action sector, which constitutes the middle sector operating *between* the public and private sectors. By definition, Uphoff says, **any organisations in the private and third sectors are non-governmental.**[16]

In an essay exploring the distinctive nature of the third sector,[17] Marc Nerfin contrasts the societal roles and orientations of the **prince** (who represents governmental power), the

---

15. The membership sector includes membership organisations (such as farmer organisations) and cooperatives. See Edwards, Michael and Hulme, David, (Eds.), "Why NGOs are not a Third Sector: a Sectoral Analysis with Some Thoughts on Accountability, Sustainability and Evaluation" by Norman Uphoff, *Non-Governmental Organisations: Performance and Accountability: Beyond the Magic Bullet,* Earthscan Publication Ltd., London, 1995, p.18.

    Membership Organisations are those organisations that are staffed and elected by the people they are meant to serve and represent. **Non-membership organisations** are, by contrast, staffed by people who are socially, professionally and at times ethnically different from their clients. See Farrington, John and Bebbington, Anthony, *Reluctant Partners? Non-Governmental Organizations, the State and Sustainable Agricultural Development*, Routledge, London and New York, 1993, p.3. For details also see Esman, M.J. and Uphoff, N., *Local Organisations: Intermediaries in rural development*, Ithaca, New York: Cornell University Press, 1984.

16. Edwards, Michael and Hulme, David (Eds.), *op. cit.*, pp. 17-18.

17. "Once the government and private business sectors are defined, scholars argue about what to call everything else. The term voluntary sector tends to imply the use of volunteers. The term **third sector** coined by Nielsen (1979) is confusing unless one already knows that government is the first sector and business the second. Although the term nonprofit sector is useful for the developed countries, it does not encompass the complex reality of the Third World today. Co-operatives, for example, promote projects benefiting an entire community, in addition to making profits for their members. Therefore, I use the term **independent sector.**" See Fisher, Julie, *op. cit.*, p.10.

merchant (representing economic power), and the **citizen** (who embodies people's power). Each is essential to the functioning of society.[18] "The prince maintains the public order. The merchant fills the need for goods and services. The responsible citizen, in association with other citizens, brings the autonomous force of people power to bear to demand the accountability of the prince and the merchant and to exercise the rights and responsibilities of citizenship."[19] Thus, Nerfin places NGOs in the **third sector** which consists of citizens and their associations.

David Korten identifies three primary types of third-party organisations in a society, viz., government, business and voluntary. He defines third parties as persons who are not themselves members of the organisation serving them; and third party organisations are those organisations which exist to serve the needs of the third parties. According to him, the roles of each of society's three third-party organisations parallel Nerfin's prince, merchant and citizen. While the legitimacy of a government organisation lies in the fact that it serves the interest of the people who reside in its jurisdiction, the social purpose of business is traced to the service of the needs of its customers. **The rationale of a voluntary organisation is based on its**

---

18. Nerfin, Marc, "Neither Prince nor Merchant – Citizen: An Introduction to the Third System", *IFDA Dossier 56*, November/December 1986, pp.3-28.
19. Korten, David C., *op. cit.*, p.96.

    "Contrasting with governmental power – the Prince – and economic power – the Merchant – there is an immediate and autonomous power, sometimes patent, always latent: people's power. Some among the people develop an awareness of this, associate and act with others and thus becomes citizens. Citizens and their associations, when they do not seek governmental or economic power, constitute the **third system.** Contributing to make patent what is latent, the third system is one expression of the autonomous power of the people." See Nerfin, Marc, *op. cit.*, pp.4-5.

functioning as an instrument of voluntary citizen in the service of a social need neglected by the prince and the merchant. When it comes to discharging responsibility, Korten adds, government does it by use of **threat power** (power of the prince) and business does it by employing **economic power** (power of the merchant), but a voluntary organisation uses **integrative power**, which is the power of the citizen.[20]

Alan Fowler offers a similar model by stating that the evolution of societies as modern nation-states gives rise to institutions and organisations established for three relatively distinct purposes:

- to protect, secure and regulate the lives and actions of citizens;
- to make a livelihood and create and accumulate wealth; and
- to pursue individual interests or tackle personal or social concerns which are separate from gaining a livelihood.

The first set of purposes typically belongs to governments (called the **government sector**), the second to business and the market (called the **business sector**), and the third to the self-willed association of citizens (called the **voluntary sector**). The size and content of the three sectors varies from country to country and each is regulated by specific regulation. Relative size is primarily determined by the political ideology dominating society, or the regime in power, etc.[21]

Classification of NGOs

The term 'NGO' embraces a wide variety of organisations. Authorities classify NGOs in different ways. However,

20. For details see Korten, David C., *op. cit.*, pp.95-96.
21. For details see Fowler, Alan, *Striking a Balance: A Guide to Enhancing the Effectiveness of Non-Governmental Organisations in International Development*, *op. cit.*, pp.20-39.

classifications of a few experts are given here which broadly includes classifications presented by other important writers on the subject.

According to David Korten,[22] NGOs include:

- **Voluntary Organisations (VOs)**[23] that pursue a social mission driven by a commitment of shared values;

---

22. Korten, David C., *op. cit.*, p.2.
23. For David Korten, "the **voluntary organisation** is the instrument through which citizen volunteers establish an identity and legal recognition for their collective endeavours. It provides their organizational support system and their means for aggregating resources for endeavours that require more than individual action. The voluntary organization, in its purist expression, exists to project the social commitment of its citizen volunteers." *Ibid.*, p.108.

    B.T. Lawani observes: "Generally, voluntary agencies and non-official organisations are treated as one and the same. This may not be so.... Voluntary organisations are spontaneous in their origin, (whereas) non-governmental agencies may be sponsored by government." See Lawani, B.T., *Non-Governmental Organizations in Development (Case Study of Solapur District)*, Rawat Publications, Jaipur and New Delhi, 1999, pp.17-18.

    The term 'voluntary' is often used to refer to services provided free by individuals working through voluntary organisations generally of a philanthropic (secular or religious) kind. One could interpret 'voluntary' in a much wider way and see it as covering any action that individuals choose to contribute for the greater social good. See Moore, David B. and Schmitz, Gerald J. (Eds.), "Can We Define the Voluntary Sector?" by Tony F. Marshall, *Debating Development Discourse (Institutional and Popular Perspectives)*, Macmillan Press Ltd., 1995, p.56.

    "The term 'voluntary' was used mainly to denote the work done by those volunteers who were not paid for. In the context of welfare activities, voluntary means those 'without the spur or compulsion of economic motives.' In other words, it is a 'self-propelled action;' self without a claim for compensation. According to P.D. Kulkarni, 'Voluntary Organisation is a native institution willed and regulated by community itself.' Herman Levin defines VO as the one in which it embodies the interest of the people through a group effort to organize

- **Public Service Contractors (PSCs)**[24] that function as market-oriented nonprofit businesses serving public purposes;
- **People's Organisations (POs)** that represent their members' interest, have member accountable leadership, and are substantially self-reliant;
- **Governmental Non-Governmental Organisations (GONGOs)** that are creations of government and serve as instruments of government policy.

---

services. VO is a legal corporate body organized by a group of persons spontaneously and governed by its own without external control or compulsion, for social welfare. We define it as a non-political, nonprofit, non-religious community organisation governed by its own rules and regulations without external control and initiated for community development." See Mathivaanan, Dr. Samuel C., *Voluntary Agencies and Social Change*, Manas Publications, 1991, p.2.

"In the Third World, the term NGO generally refers to organizations involved in development, broadly defined. Hospitals, charitable organizations, and universities are usually called voluntary or nonprofit organizations rather than NGOs." See Fisher, Julie, *op. cit.*, p.5.

"We can think of four types of voluntary associations: (a) those whose policy and programmes confront the state apparatus; (b) those whose actions are different from the state apparatus; (c) those which are recognized by state apparatus; and (d) those instituted by state apparatus." See Kapoor, A.K. and Singh, Dharamvir, *Rural Development through NGOs*, Rawat Publications, 1997, p.13.

24. "Business may be either for-profit or nonprofit. There are many nonprofit organizations that measure their performance primarily in financial terms and that are as market oriented as any business in their approach to determining what products and messages will sell to...donors. Nonprofit organizations that are in the business of selling their services to private contributors and government agencies to implement public purposes as defined by those contributors or agencies are part of a sub-class of business organization known as public service contractors. The customer in this instance is the donor." See Korten, David C., *op. cit.*, p.97.

Julie Fisher includes four major types of organisations as NGOs:[25]

(i) **Grassroots Organisations (GROs)**: These are membership organisations that work to improve and develop their own communities' also called *People's Organisations* or *base groups*. There are **three major types of GROs**:

- **Local development associations**, such as village councils or neighbourhood associations. They work on many development issues that concern the entire community and represent an entire community.
- **Interest associations** are more limited in membership and tend to work on particular issues. These include women's groups, water users association, and shared work groups. They represent a particular group within a community.
- **Pre-cooperatives and cooperatives, and other community-based enterprises** are the third type of GRO. Their service is profit based. Cooperatives can have a major impact on developing their own communities, yet they clearly differ from nonprofit GROs, as well as from private businesses without members.

(ii) **Grassroots Support Organisations (GRSOs)**: These are nationally or regionally based *development assistance organisations*, usually composed of paid professionals that work with GROs in communities other than their own. Some observers call these *intermediary NGOs*.[26]

---

25. Fisher, Julie, *op. cit.*, pp. 4, 6 and 191-192.

26. "A new form of organization has been emerging among the voluntary development organizations.... These have been variously called Support Organizations, Resource Organizations, Intermediary Organizations, etc. These organizations essentially provide support to strengthen the work of grassroots voluntary development organizations, peoples' movements and other individuals engaged in voluntary development initiatives. The various functions played by such organizations include research, training, advocacy, technical assistance,

(iii) **Grassroots Organisations (GRO) Networks:** GRO Networks imply horizontal linkages among GROs that are regionally based. These networks link local communities to one another.

(iv) **Grassroots Support Organisations (GRSO) Networks:** These are based on horizontal linkages among GRSOs and include formal *umbrella organisations* or *consortia*, *informal service networks* that exchange expertise and cooperate in the field, and broader *support movements* that may include individual professionals and activists as well as GROs.

Rajesh Tandon has discussed following four broad types of NGOs in his book, *NGO-Government Relations: A Source of Life or A Kiss of Death*:[27]

Type A: Service Providers: Service Providing NGOs are inspired by welfare concerns, and they largely provide services to the poor.

---

information dissemination, documentation, etc." See *Voluntary Development Organizations in India: A Study of History, Roles and Future Challenges*, November 1991, Society for Participatory Research in Asia, New Delhi, p.39.

27. For details see Tandon, Rajesh, *op. cit.*, pp.9-12.

In an exercise to map the diversity of voluntary sector in India, Rajesh Tandon has provided the following typology of civil society associations in the Indian context. **Traditional Associations:** Such associations exist around a social unit either defined by a tribe, ethnicity or caste. Associations of this variety undertake a wide range of functions in the lives of those citizens. Besides mediating inter-family relations, such associations develop elaborate systems, norms and procedures for governing the use and protection of natural resources. **Religious Associations:** Charity, help to the needy, service to the poor and *daan* (giving) have been uniformly recommended by all the religions and sects in India. Education, health care, drinking water, afforestation, social welfare, etc. are numerous arenas of human action where fairly organised forms of civil society activity are carried out by religiously inspired voluntary organisations. **Social Movements:** In the

Type B: Empowerment NGOs: Empowerment NGOs are development oriented NGOs who work on empowerment or work through educational intervention in certain developmental sectors.

Type C: Support NGOs: They are newly emerging NGOs who provide a variety of support functions to different grass-roots NGOs.

Type D: Umbrella or Network NGOs: The 1980s mark the rise of networks of NGOs, and umbrella or federation type NGOs. The networks are more informal, limited purpose and, therefore, time-bound associations of NGOs coming together to work on a common issue.

According to John Clark, NGOs do not comprise a tight community but a broad spectrum. The spectrum does not divide

---

contemporary Indian context, a number of social movements, spear-headed by social movement organisations have emerged as major manifestations of civil society. These movements are of several types: focusing on the interest and aspirations of particular groups (such as SCs, STs and women); protests against social evils (like liquor, dowry, inheritance rights etc); protests against displacement due to big development projects; campaigns against environmental degradation, corruption and for rights to information, education and livelihood. VOs/NGOs through the social movements try to reform society, institutions and governance and act as harbingers of social change. **Membership Associations:** Membership organisations may be representational set-up to represent the opinions and interest of a particular category of citizens e.g. unions of rural labour, farm workers, women workers, consumer associations etc., professional – formed around a particular occupation or profession, e.g., association of lawyers, teachers, engineers, managers, journalists, etc. Self Help Groups are a growing category of membership organisations. **Intermediary Associations:** These associations function between individual citizens and macro state institutions like the bureaucracy, judiciary and police etc. These could be of several types, e.g. service delivery, mobilisation, support, philanthropic, advocacy and network. For details see Tandon, Rajesh, "Civil Society in India: An Exercise in Mapping," *Innovations in Civil Society*, Volume 1, No.1, July 2001, pp.2-9.

precisely into separate primary colours. Most are mixtures, a blend of several of the colors on the pallet, though one may predominate. NGOs, reflecting largely their historical evolution, can be divided into six schools. They are as under:[28]

Relief and Welfare Agencies: such as Catholic Relief Services, various missionary societies and so on.

Technical Innovation Organisations: NGOs that operate their own projects to pioneer new or improved approaches to problems, and which tend to remain specialised in their chosen field.

Public Service Contractors: NGOs that are mostly funded by Northern governments and that work closely with southern governments and official aid agencies. These NGOs are contracted to implement components of official programmes because it is felt that their size and flexibility would help them perform the tasks more effectively than government departments.

Popular Development Agencies: Northern NGOs and their southern intermediary counterparts that concentrate on self-help, social development and grassroots democracy.

Grassroots Development Organisations: Locally based southern NGOs whose members are the poor and oppressed themselves, and which attempt to shape a popular development process. They often receive support from popular development agencies, though many receive no external funding at all.

Advocacy Groups and Networks: Organisations that have no field projects but exist primarily for education and lobbying.

"The World Bank distinguishes between two main groups of NGOs – **Operational NGOs (ONGOs)** and **Advocacy NGOs (ANGOs)**. However, it does not view these distinctions as rigid and recognises that the majority of NGOs operate along a

---

28. Clark, John, *op. cit.*, pp.34-35.

continuum in which a great deal of overlap exists. For instance, many operational NGOs are active players in national and international policy fora and can also undertake an advocacy role with partners as borrower governments and the Bank in the context of program implementation."[29]

Taxonomy of NGOs

Based on the understanding of the definitions of NGOs and their clones, an attempt has been made here to draw a taxonomic chart of NGOs that looks like reconciling many controversies on the subject. It combines the major streams of thought on definition of NGO.

As per the taxonomy, NGOs are of two types – Non-Developmental NGOs (NDNGOs) and developmental NGOs or Non-Government Developmental Organisations (NGDOs). The NGDOs are of five types – Voluntary Organisations (VOs), Public Service Contractors (PSCs), People's Organisations (POs) or Grassroots Organisations (GROs), Governmental Non-Governmental Organisations (GONGOs), Grassroots Support Organisations (GRSOs). POs or GROs are further divided into three types of organisations, namely, Local Development Associations (LDAs), Precooperatives/Co-operatives, etc., Interest Associations. VOs, PSCs and POs together form GRO networks and GRSOs constitute GRSO networks.

The definitions of the terms accepted for the purpose of this taxonomy are as follows. While **NGOs** are taken as organisations that are non-governmental in nature, **NDNGOs** stand broadly for private sector business organisations (termed non-developmental for the reason that their existence is primarily commercial and their developmental role, if any, is

29. *The World Bank's Partnership with Nongovernmental Organisations (Participation and NGO Group – Poverty and Social Policy Department)*, The World Bank, May 1996, p.4.

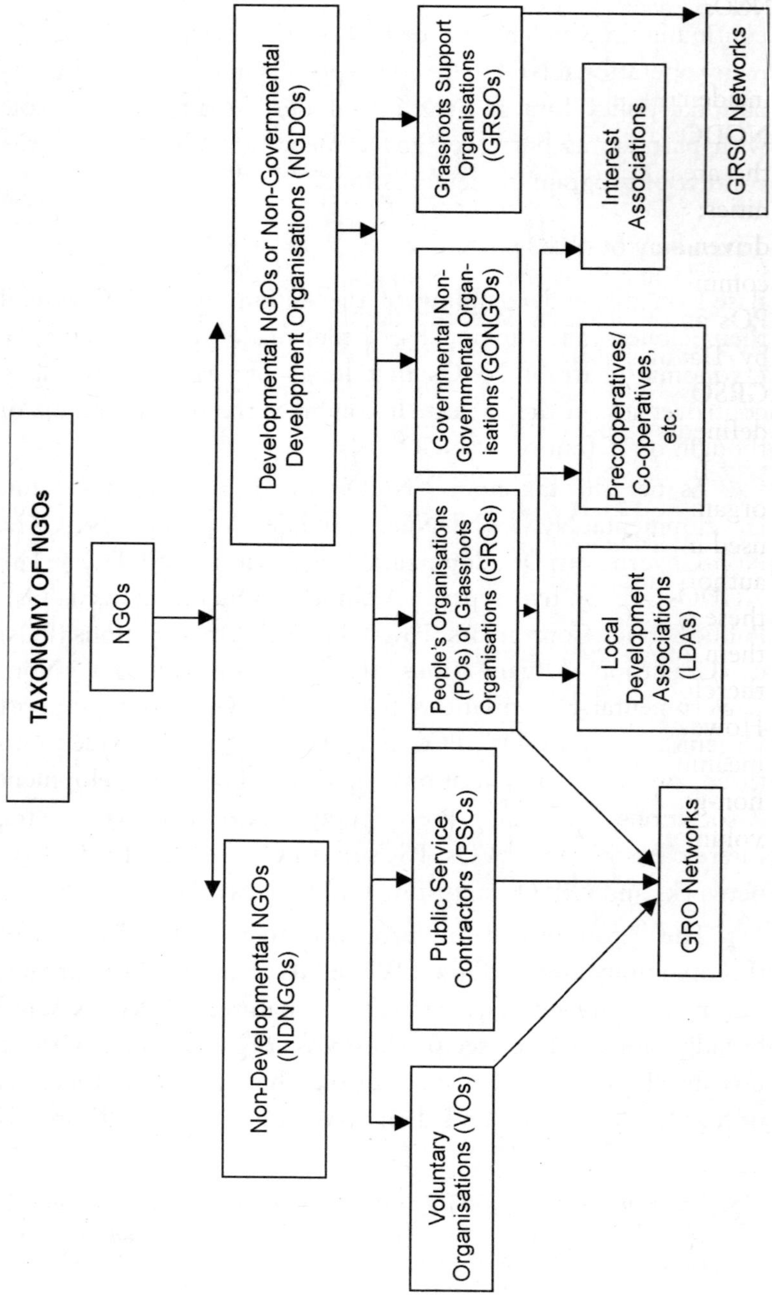
TAXONOMY OF NGOs
NGOs
Developmental NGOs or Non-Governmental Development Organisations (NGDOs)
Non-Developmental NGOs (NDNGOs)
Grassroots Support Organisations (GRSOs)
Governmental Non-Governmental Organisations (GONGOs)
People's Organisations (POs) or Grassroots Organisations (GROs)
Public Service Contractors (PSCs)
Voluntary Organisations (VOs)
GRSO Networks
Interest Associations
Precooperatives/ Co-operatives, etc.
Local Development Associations (LDAs)
GRO Networks

incidental) and non-developmental non-business organisations; **NGDOs** are development-oriented NGOs working primarily in the areas relating to socio-economic development of communities; **VOs** are those organisations that pursue a social mission driven by a commitment of shared values and project the social commitment of its citizen volunteers. The definitions of **PSCs**, **POs** and **GONGOs** accepted for this taxonomy are as defined by David Korten, and the definitions of the terms **GROs**, **GRSOs**, **GRO networks** and **GRSO networks** are taken as defined by Julie Fisher.

In the pages ahead, the terms NGO, NGDO, voluntary organisation and voluntary development organisation are often used interchangeably, depending upon the ideas borrowed from authors and authorities with their own preferences in using these terms. As is understood, the line of difference between them on many an occasion is non-existent or very thin, and therefore, apparently insignificant for the purpose of this work. However, while using the terms in the upcoming chapters the meaning carried is that NGOs are ordinarily nonprofit, non-government or remotely government like GONGOs, voluntary, development organisations.

2

NGOs: Growth

Kill the spirit of voluntarism in man, you kill his life's essence. In other words, with the death of voluntarism, God ceases to dwell in man.

– ***Author's reflection***

Why NGO Boom

The neo-classical economics or the theory of modernisation developed from industrial success in Europe. The theory owes much to the anti-Marxist ideas of the American economist W.W. Rostow, who propounded five stages of the process of development: traditional; pre-conditions for take-off; take-off into self-sustaining growth; drive to maturity; age of mass-consumption. The model suggested that development trickles down to the subsistence sector through *free market forces*.[1] But, in Africa, and for most of Asia, the trickle has been too small to be noticeable. The ideas of modernists have had a

1. For details see Rostow, W.W., *The Stages of Economic Growth: A Non-Communist Manifesto*. London: Longman Inc. 1960.

negative effect on rural development. Trickle-down is discredited. **The current boom in NGOs can be attributed partly to a reaction against the neo-classical modernists.**[2]

According to Riddel and Robinson, the growth in the number of NGOs in development has been "due partly to the increase in official funding," and "also to the changing, and increasingly positive, perceptions of the public at large, who have significantly increased their contributions to the NGO movement.... Partly, too, the growth of NGOs has occurred as a result of the failure of official aid programmes to reach down and assist the poor, and partly because of donor pressure on recipient governments to reduce their direct involvement in development programmes...."[3]

Growth of NGOs in World Arena

In the areas of poverty alleviation, eradication of hunger, protecting the environment, grassroots development and safeguarding the poor from the debt crisis the official agencies have limited experience or encounter tremendous operational difficulties. This has led the governments to actively seek the collaboration of both northern and southern NGOs, which have reputation for working in the areas of great poverty, having direct relationships with the communities of poor people

---

2. Poulton, Robin and Harris, Michael (Eds.), *"On Charities and NGOs by Michael Harris," Putting People First: Voluntary Organisations and Third World Development*, Macmillan, 1988, pp.12-14.

   Harris further adds that NGOs have now anchored themselves to Adam Smith's analysis that a necessary prerequisite for industrial revolution was an agricultural revolution. The NGO movement now apparently aims at self-sufficiency, and a better life for the rural poor; it seeks an upgrading of methods which make possible an indigenous agricultural revolution. *Ibid.*, p.14.

3. Riddel, Roger and Robinson, Mark, *Non-Governmental Organizations and Rural Poverty Alleviation*, Overseas Development Institute, London, Clarendon Press, Oxford, 1995, p.2.

and considerable experience in tackling environmental problems.[4]

Voluntary organisations in different guises existed well before the twentieth century in both North and South, and NGOs, as they are recognised today, have a more recent history.[5] During the last few decades, there has been increased visibility and reference to the work of voluntary organisations in the development discourse. The 1980s can be characterised as discovering the role, potential and limitations of the work of voluntary development organisations in developing and developed countries of the world. While the existence of voluntary organisations in certain parts of the world had been a long standing historical phenomenon, in some parts (like Latin America) they emerged quite recently, i.e., within the last four decades.[6]

In the modern times, the first northern NGOs to enter the stage did so just after the First World War, such as the Catholic Church-based CARITAS and Save the Children Fund. They gained strength towards the end of, and immediately after, the Second World War. Hence, OXFAM started in 1942, Catholic Relief Services in 1943, and the Co-operative for American

---

4. Clark, John, *Democratizing Development: The Role of Voluntary Organizations*, Kumarian Press, 1991, pp.4-5.

   In Mozambique some 120 national and international NGOs dominate welfare services and in Kampuchea the NGOs are the main development partners of the government. In Brazil, grassroots organisations working with the rubber tappers and the tribal Indians have over the years shifted their government away from its indifference to environmentalism. In the Philippines environmental organisations have succeeded in arresting the breakneck logging by huge timber concerns in the island of Palawan. *Ibid.*

5. *Ibid.*, p.29.

6. Tandon, Rajesh, *NGO-Government Relations: A Source of Life or A Kiss of Death*, Society for Participatory Research in Asia, New Delhi, p.3.

Relief Everywhere (CARE) in 1945. Initially, these NGOs were engaged in relief work, primarily in war-torn Europe.[7] The beginning of relief agencies world over was mostly Church-inspired. It was the Christian spirit of duty and compassion that were most often the guiding lights. **In this secular age the Christian spirit is not a fashionable reference point but its creation of the voluntary development movement cannot be ignored.**[8]

The NGO pursuing relief as their primary role gradually shifted their attention to the Third World and also broadened its focus to include welfare activities. When Leslie Kirkley joined Oxfam as chief executive in 1951, he gave emphasis to the growing belief that **prevention is better than cure.** It was Ritchie Caider who gave publicity to the saying **"Give a man a fish and you feed him for today – teach him how to fish and he feeds himself and his family for the rest of their lives."**[9] One result of this was that the long-term aid changed to development, particularly, through NGO.[10] This was the trend with most of the NGOs of 1950s and 1960s.[11]

At the start of this period development work fitted into a conventional 'modernising' school of thought, helping poor

---

7. Clark, John, *op. cit.*, p.29.
8. Poulton, Robin and Harris, Michael (Eds.), *op. cit.*, p.5.
9. Originally said by Lao Tse, Taoist philosopher c. 600 B.C. of China.
10. Poulton, Robin and Harris, Michael (Eds.), *op. cit.*, p.1.
11. "During the 1950s and 1960s the number of Northern NGOs multiplied and their focus moved progressively into development activities. They saw that relief attacked only the symptoms of poverty. To attack deprivation itself necessitated helping the poor increase their capacity to meet their own needs with the resources they control. The shift of location from the refugee camps, feeding centers and hospitals to the villages and slums where they set about establishing their projects opened the northern NGOs eyes to the full reality of poverty...." Clark, John, *op. cit.*, pp.29-30.

communities to become more like northern societies by importing northern ideas, technology and expertise. Gradually, many NGOs came to criticise the negative effects of the traditional development model. **They started to shift to a new role, that of providing a service to the popular grassroots organisations.** The increased funding opportunities from northern voluntary sources led to a mushrooming of southern NGOs. Many of these grew rapidly to become national-level institutions, which served as intermediate organisations, channelling assistance from the northern NGO to the grassroots level. New political concepts emerging from Third World intellectuals, such as the theology of liberation, also greatly influenced NGO thinking during this period. Development theory, once dominated by northern practitioners, was becoming an indigenous process, led by the people themselves.[12]

In the 1970s, many NGOs engaged in self-help activities came to realise that there was a limit to how far self-help activities could go. Development was increasingly viewed as a process of liberating the poor. Meanwhile, Brazilian NGOs pioneered the approach of **'conscientisation'** designed to improve living standards, to help the poor to perceive their exploitation and realise the opportunities they have for overcoming such exploitation through mass organisation. The realisation that **poverty is political in nature** also gave birth to advocacy by NGOs. They began programmes of development education, public campaigning and parliamentary lobbying in pursuit of political changes.[13]

The 1980s saw an important leap forward in advocacy. The Northern NGOs with overseas programmes, through their

---

12. *Ibid.*, p.30.
13. *Ibid.*, p.31.

Conscientisation is a combination of political education, social organisation and grassroots development. *Ibid.*

advocacy work, achieved a great deal because of their credibility with the public and with governments. Most importantly, a number of parallel advocacy groups emerged in the Third World. North-South networks of advocacy groups increased the authenticity, analytical strength and power of NGO advocacy by several orders of magnitude.[14]

In the 1990s and after, the NGO trend is influencing change in southern official structures. David Korten calls it **micro-policy reform.** Micro-policy reform involves creation of new institutions (e.g., to provide credit to the poor), mammoth retraining exercises (e.g., to redirect agricultural extension services) and wholesale changes in attitudes (e.g., to dismantle the barriers that hold women in a second-class status). The reform of this nature is an enormous task, but the potential benefit for the poor is revolutionary. In their search for political influence, NGOs increasingly look beyond their national boundaries and opt for networking.[15]

The central agenda of the period is one of **innovation and change**: in values, institutions and technologies. Such change is visible in the realm of civil society, but most particularly in the voluntary sector. The existing institutions are creations of the past; if transformation is to come to these institutions, it must come as a consequence of voluntary action. **Voluntary action was at the heart of the reform movements that swept the socialist countries of Eastern Europe.** In the West, US President George Bush is talking about *a thousand points of light* – the work of countless citizen volunteers – as the potential hope for a solution to America's social ills. Apparently, the world has to steer its course through voluntarism in the coming years to

14. *Ibid.*, pp.31-32.
15. *Ibid.*, pp.33 and 6-7.

remove the long-standing social and economic problems of the human race.[16]

Growth of NGOs in India

NGOs existed much before the most governments, though they were known by other names.[17] History has tangible linkages with voluntarism and voluntary action since the beginning of the 19th century.[18] In India, steeped in the tradition of philosophy and humanism, people of eminence built lasting institutions enlisting public co-operation and promoting ideas of charity, love and brotherhood.[19] The scale and pace with which NGOs have grown during 1980s and 1990s have no match in the past. They take up functions in new areas, such as economic uplift or development of deprived classes, compared to their traditional concern for relief and welfare. They have become internally sophisticated, better organised and more aware of their power, and thus have turned more militant as well as capable in mobilisation activities. Despite their exponential growth over a long period the NGO curve is still rising.[20]

---

16. Korten, David C., *Getting to the 21st Century: Voluntary Action and the Global Agenda*, Kumarian Press, 1990, pp.105-106.
17. Cernea, Michael M., 40, *World Bank Discussion Papers–Nongovernmental Organizations and Local Development*, The World Bank, Washington D.C., 1988, p.2.
18. Kapoor, A.K. and Singh, Dharamvir, *Rural Development through NGOs*, Rawat Publications, 1997, p.15.
19. Mouli, V. Chandra (Ed.), *Role of Voluntary Organisations in Rural Development*, Sterling Publishers Pvt. Ltd., 1990, p.28.
20. Cernea, Michael M., *op. cit.*, pp.2-3.

    "...keeping in view the magnitude of growth of these organizations in recent years, even a conservative rough estimate of the number of voluntary organizations both registered and unregistered in the entire country, may work out to anywhere between 25,000 to 30,000." See Mouli, V. Chandra (Ed.), *op. cit.*, pp.28-29.

The early southern NGOs typically arose out of independence struggles.[21] In India they had deeper roots. "The foundations for the contemporary voluntary agency movement were laid in the pre-independence period, some of them were associated with the **social reform movements** of the late 19th century, largely concerned with educational and cultural matters and only tangentially with the question of poverty. **Christian missionary groups** established a network of hospitals, schools, and welfare service for the poor in the first half of the twentieth century. A third tradition was the **Gandhian approach,** which combined social reform with village development activities."[22] It is also said that the genesis of voluntary organisation movement in India has been in the "people's participation" in various stages to eradicate poverty, and this participation is called by various names, such as popular participation, people's institution, self-help groups, functional groups, etc.[23]

The Gandhian way of service had many offshoots that still flourish today, like handloom and appropriate technology centres, schools for functional education, People's Courts that

---

"In the absence of any census of these NGOs, it is difficult to give any accurate number. But there were approximately 10,000 NGOs aided by the Central Social Welfare Board in its earlier years. Currently, the tentative estimate of all NGOs engaged...in all types of developmental activities is around 50,000." See Nanavathy, Meher and Kulkarni, P.D., *NGOs in the Changing Scenario*, Uppal Publishing House, 1998, p.3.

21. *Non-Governmental Organisations and Micro-Entrepreneurship Development (Evolution and Strategies),* Aseed, School of Entrepreneurship Management, 1992, p.2.
22. Riddel, Roger and Robinson, Mark, *op. cit.*, p.140.
23. *Non-Governmental Organisations and Micro-Entrepreneurship Development (Evolution and Strategies),* Aseed School of Entrepreneurship Management, 1992, p.2.

use nonviolent citizens' pressure to achieve justice, etc.[24] Mahatma Gandhi made a major attempt to harness and channelise people's participation. Central to his approach was the value of giving. There were two types of gifts: **individual gift**, of which *Bhoodaan* and *Shramdaan* were two examples; and **community gift** – for example, *Gramdaan*. Through *Gramdaan* village people used to offer their lands to the village assembly, i.e., *Gram Sabha*.[25]

The history of voluntary movement since the 19th century can be divided into eight phases. The first half of the 19th century (1800-1850) constituted the **first phase** during which Indian history was marked by social reform movements in the wake of the introduction of ideas and thoughts of the West, besides including Christian missionary activities. The work of Christian missionaries in modern times practically begun with the 18th century, but the East Indian Company at that time had restricted the operation of missionaries from their territory. The Charter Act of 1813 removed all restrictions on missionary activities in India, and provided for the maintenance and support of a Church establishment in British India. This led to expansion of missionary work in a big way in the area already conquered by the British. In remote and secluded tribal areas, missionaries contributed a great deal by providing for their "self-conceptualisation and self-esteem" as communities.

---

24. Clark, John, *Ibid.*, p.29.
25. *Non-Governmental Organisations and Micro-Entrepreneurship Development (Evolution and Strategies), op. cit.*, p.3.

    Another set of voluntary organisations are those set up by established business and industrial houses in India. Historically, they have played a role in charity. Education and health have been the sectors of focus. During the last 30 years or so, some of them have started rural development projects. In recent years, these organisations have been criticized as instruments to siphon-off funds by the rich from their existing business incomes to avoid paying income tax. See Kapoor, A.K. and Singh, Dharamvir, *op. cit.*, p.23.

Though the primary objective of the operations of missionaries was the spread of faith, with a view to achieving their objective "they approached people through services such as education and health."[26]

The **second phase** spanned from 1850 to 1900. Drain of resources, creation of communication links, setting up of jute and cotton mills, spread of English education were the highlights of this period that directly or indirectly contributed to institutionalised movements*. During this phase spread of nationalism and self-help emerged as the primary focus of socio-political movements that influenced the future course of voluntary action.[27]

The **third phase** continued up to India's Independence. The major factor in this phase that influenced the area of voluntary action has been the successful attempt of channelling the voluntary spirit for political action and mass mobilisation for Independence. The second factor was Gandhi's initiation of 'constructive work'.[28]

The **fourth phase** of voluntary initiatives started after Independence.[29] Soon after independence, the approach of

---

26. Kapoor, A.K. and Singh, Dharamvir, *Ibid.*, pp.15-16.
27. *Ibid.*, p.17.

* e.g., Satyasodhak Samaj (1873), Arya Samaj (1875), Brahmo Samaj (1878), Indian National Social Reform Association (1897) and Ramakrishna Mission (1898). The Indian National Congress came up as an official platform for the expression of growing national consciousness in 1885. *Ibid.*

28. *Ibid.*, pp.18-19.
29. *Ibid.*, p.19.

In 1947, there were quite a few voluntary service organisations, some of them with a fairly long standing. But most of them – barring a few Gandhian organisations engaged in what Gandhiji called constructive work – were in the urban areas. But then in the following decades voluntary organisations multiplied fast all over the country. This was partly due to the euphoria generated by the newly acquired

mixed economy was adopted by the government, in terms of which certain sectors were controlled by the state, and the rest were left to the people. The underlying principle of this strategy allowed people's participation in various spheres of economic activity. In 1952, the Community Development Programme was launched. The policy of people's participation with an active role for bureaucracy was the moot point of the programme.[30] Provision of welfare services was a co-operative venture between the state and voluntary organisations since the time of the First Five-Year Plan.[31] The First Five-Year Plan document stated, *inter alia*, that a "major responsibility for organizing activities in different fields of social welfare...falls naturally on private voluntary agencies.... Any plan for social and economic regeneration should take into account the services rendered by these agencies and the State should give them maximum co-operation in strengthening their efforts." To promote voluntary action a special autonomous body, Central Social Welfare Board, was set up during the First Plan.[32] In the stream of reform-based voluntary action and constructive work many people joined in the task of nation-building of the government during the period upto mid-sixties.[33] "The Christian and Gandhian approaches continued to predominate after Independence. In the early post-Independence period, disaster relief and food-for-work programmes came to be associated with Christian organisations in particular. Social welfare

---

independence and partly due to the declared availability of government grants introduced under the successive Five-Year plans. See Nanavathy, Meher and Kulkarni, P.D., *op. cit.*, p.3.

30. *Non-Governmental Organisations and Micro-Entrepreneurship Development (Evolution and Strategies)*, Aseed, School of Entrepreneurship Management, 1992, p.3.
31. Mathivaanan, Dr. Samuel C., *Voluntary Agencies and Social Change*, Manas Publications, 1991, p.14.
32. *Ibid.*
33. Kapoor, A.K. and Singh, Dharamvir, *op. cit.*, p.19.

provided critical back-up for public service provision in the 1950s and early 1960s, and agencies steeped in Gandhian values emphasized village self-reliance and provided the foundation for development activities centred on small-scale agriculture and cottage industry."[34]

The **fifth phase** formed the period between the mid-sixties to the early seventies. This was the time when failure of the development model followed by the government came to be noticed. It was at this stage that the integrated rural development approach was experimented. The liberation of Bangladesh and the gigantic task of rehabilitation of refugees and the people of Bangladesh also saw many young people join this effort. This was also the period when the Naxalite movement surfaced and gained momentum and reached its peak. A small number of new professionally trained young persons began to enter voluntary development organisations, setting up new initiatives located close to big cities.[35] The integrated development approach became popular in the late 1960s and early 1970s, with NGOs combining health and education with economic programmes in pursuit of poverty alleviation. It was also at this time that funding from international NGOs started to make its mark.[36]

The **sixth phase** lasted up to 1979. The 'restless many' looking for constructive alternatives started to channelise their energies and concerns towards realising their dream of a more humane and just society. The fallout of the political process contributed to the growth in voluntary action, both in terms of quality and quantity. The ideas about conscientisation and people's participation began to emerge in Indian NGOs. With the growth in the number and scope of voluntary agencies,

34. Riddel, Roger and Robinson, Mark, *op. cit.*, p.140.
35. Kapoor, A.K. and Singh, Dharamvir, *op. cit.*, pp. 20-21.
36. Riddel, Roger and Robinson, Mark, *op. cit.*, p.140.

sector-based specialisation in work of the agencies gained momentum.[37] "During the latter half of the 1970s, a more radical trend emerged, with social action groups, taking the view that poverty was a structural phenomenon. They abjured violence but the thrust of their activities was confrontational, initiating struggles over issues such as land reform, wages, and bonded labour, while another dimension of their work rested on empowering the poor to demand efficient delivery of services from the State and pressing for the implementation of progressive components of government legislation. With liberal foreign funding, social action groups proliferated throughout the late 1970s and early 1980s, and established themselves as the dominant type of NGO in some states."[38]

The phase of the eighties, termed as the **seventh phase,** witnessed a growth in voluntary action in the form of support organisations specialising in training, research, advocacy, documentations, legal aid, etc. Issues like women's development, environment, forestry, began to gain significance. The work of voluntary organisations also began to get organised around issues and campaigns related to droughts, water pollution, etc. Recognition and visibility of the work of voluntary organisations increased.[39] The fundamental objectives

---

37. Mathivaanan, Dr. Samuel C., *op. cit.*, p.21.
38. *Ibid.*
39. Kapoor, A.K. and Singh, Dharamvir, *op. cit.*, p.22.

    From the mid-1980s, a further trend emerged within the NGO movement, emphasizing the importance of a professional approach based on sound management, planning, and co-ordination. A parallel development was the creation of resource agencies which work directly with the poor and provide support services to other NGOs in the form of training, evaluation, and documentation. These agencies are usually financed, among others, by core grants from foreign donors. Intermediary agencies responsible for channeling funds from foreign donors to small national NGOs in some cases also provide these types of services, for example, in assisting with evaluations. See Riddel, Roger and Robinson, Mark, *op. cit.*, p.141.

of NGO activity in rural India were poverty alleviation and the empowerment of the poor, primarily through small-scale development projects. Some NGOs had chosen to tackle the symptoms of poverty manifested in low educational standards, ill-health, poor sanitation, and inferior housing by means of social welfare programmes. An alternative approach had been for NGOs to empower poor people to demand resources from the state or to challenge injustice and exploitation.[40]

During the nineties, considered as the **eighth phase**, NGOs "have emerged as important players in the development arena. On the one hand, voluntary sector is making significant contributions at the UN sponsored meetings at global level, and on the other, VOs are also working for the empowerment of the poor at the grassroots level and are providing quick help in the management of disasters. Role of VOs was particularly recognised at the United Nations Conference on Environment and Development held at Rio de Janeiro, Brazil in June 1992. Thereafter, active presence of VOs continued at all important global international fora, such as the Cairo Population Conference 1994, the Copenhagen World Summit on Social Development 1995, the Beijing Conference on Women 1995, and so on." The 1980s and 1990s are called the periods of NGO boom in the country.[41]

In India, voluntarism started as social work with a focus on charity, but it has now veered towards developmental work and community mobilisation. Accessibility to centers of power and ability of the leaders to secure men, material and resources are mainly responsible for having voluntary organisations in rural areas.[42]

---

40. *Ibid.*
41. *Report of the Steering Committee on Voluntary Sector for the Tenth Five-Year Plan (2002-2007)*, Planning Commission, Government of India, January 2002, pp.3-4.
42. Kapoor, A.K. and Singh, Dharamvir, *Op. Cit.*, p.24.

3

NGOs: Structure

Law ordinarily implies control which corrupts systems and thereby the life of people in badly governed states. Laws controlling the voluntary sector are prone to build more nexus of the government and the nongovernment and corrupt the voluntary sector more.

– *Author's reflection*

Structure Defined

The Concise Oxford Dictionary of Current English defines *structure* as "a set of interconnecting parts of any complex thing".[1] Although scholars differ on many questions on the subject of organisation, there is a reasonable consensus on what is meant by structure itself.[2] Litterer, in his widely read book on organisations, writes: "**By structure we mean the identification of the elements in an organization and relations between**

1. *The Concise Oxford Dictionary of Current English,* Ninth Edition, Oxford University Press, New Delhi, 1995, p.1382.
2. Edwards, Michael and Fowler, Alan (Eds.), "Strategy and Structure in Managing Global Associations", by Young, Dennis R., Koenig, Bonnie L., Najam, Adil and Fisher, Julie, *The Earthscan Reader on NGO Management*, Earthscan, 2003, p.166.

them."[3] Ben-Ner, Montias and Neuberger[4] identify Litterer's **elements** in terms of **groups of people** within organisations and his **relations** in terms of the patterns of **resource allocation, authority, incentives, division of work, and information** that connect and coordinate them within organisations. A.D. Chandler in his work 'Scale and Scope' specifically focuses on **the design of organisation** through which the enterprise is administered.[5]

NGO Structure Defined

Alan Fowler has devised a model of NGO structure applicable universally to NGOs. The framework reflects key characteristics of NGOs. It concentrates on areas which are critical to their work and their role in society. As he says, "to do development well, NGOs must have adequate capacity in five areas; each must be consistent with the other. The first two relate to an **organisational design** and **systems** *which link vision to action through appropriate development strategies, programmes and projects*; these are carried out by competent and well-managed people. The next three capacities link the NGO to the outside world by mobilising necessary **resources**; maintaining a variety of external **relationships**; and producing **results** consistent with

---

3. Litterer, J.A. (Ed.), *Organizations, Vol. I,* John Wiley and Sons, Inc., New York, 1969, p.11.
4. Ben-Ner, A., Montias, J.M., and Neuberger, E., "Basic issues in Organizations: A Comparative Perspective", *Journal of Comparative Economics*, Vol. 17, 1993, pp.207-242.
5. For details see Chandler, A.D., *Scale and Scope*, Harvard University Press, Cambridge, Massachusetts, 1990.

   Structure is the arrangement, architecture or design of an organisation that includes relationships of roles in the organisation, its formal committees, policies, procedures, rules and regulations. See Chadha, Prem, Jagadananda, and Lal, Gayatri, *Organizational Behaviour: A Framework for Non-Government Development Organizations*, CYSD, 2003, p.92.

the mission." Thus, Fowler's NGO framework consists of the following parts: vision (emanating from the society), mission, strategy, programmes, projects, people, structure, systems, management, resources, relationships, and results and learning (to impact the society).[6]

In keeping with the analysis of structure and various facets of the NGO framework, we may now proceed to examine, among other things, organisational vision, mission, strategy, registration and management structure with emphasis on nature of the NGO structure as are found in practice in India.

Organisational Vision

In the words of Alan Fowler, an organisation's vision is its view of how it would perceive the world to be, its hopes for **'reality to be'** as opposed to the **'reality that is'.** Visions are expressions of ideals, and may not be attainable in one lifetime or even in many lifetimes.[7] Organisational visions often originate from an individual vision founder, or from a group of people who have certain ideas about how life could be made better than what it actually is. Visions are the lifeblood of effective development organisations. A clearly articulated vision can provide

---

6. For details see Fowler, Alan, *Striking a Balance: A Guide to Enhancing the Effectiveness of Non-Governmental Organisations in International Development*, Earthscan Publications Ltd., London, 1997, pp.43-68.

   The NGO structure consists of **structure characteristics,** such as technical automation, differentiation and integration mechanisms including formal relationships, and hierarchy and centralization-decentralization, **financial systems, project monitoring and evaluation systems,** and **administrative support mechanisms.** For details see Chadha, Prem, Jagadananda and Lal, Gayatri, *op. cit.*, p.96.

7. For details see Fowler, Alan, "Organisational Vision, Mission, and Strategic Planning", (Paper presented during Development Management Course at PRIA), New Delhi, 1997.

momentum and strength to individuals working in development organisations.[8]

Organisational Mission

An organisational mission describes the organisation's manner of realising its vision. If an organisation's vision is to create a world where no child ever dies of a preventable disease, its mission would be some thing like providing health services to women and children in areas lacking in it. A clear mission connects the vision to a method for achieving that vision. The mission can guide an organisation's leaders in policy decisions. It helps define both what the organisations will do and what it won't do. The mission keeps the organisation focused and effective.[9]

Organisational Strategy

After the mission is articulated, the need arises to elaborate how the organisation is going to accomplish it. This means that there is a need to spell out the strategy which is appropriate for moving in the direction set by the mission. A strategy is a set of

---

8. Bhose, Joel S.G.R., *NGOs and Rural Development: Theory and Practice*, Concept Publishing Company, New Delhi, 2003, p.41.
9. *Ibid.*, p.42.

Strategic **vision** has an illusionary quality. A visionary leader wants to make her vision one with the organisational life, which she attempts through the intermediary called **mission**. It is this illusionary character of the visionary's vision that makes it hard to sustain over time. NGDOs being *process* organisations (as opposed to being *product* organisations), their processes are very intangible and mutable. It is, therefore, very hard to sustain and conserve organisational visions and missions through such evanescent processes. For details see Chadha, Prem, Jagadananda and Lal, Gayatri, *op. cit.*, p.21-22.

Mission is the purpose for which an NGDO has come into existence or continues to exist and the commitment to certain ideals or vision that an NGDO aims to fulfill. *Ibid.*, p.272.

concepts that guide an organisation's use of its resources to pursue its mission. Embedded in a strategy are answers to the following questions: What is the nature of the development problems the organisation seeks to solve? How will the activities of the organisation contribute to substantial and sustainable change in those problems? How can the organisation use its strengths and avoid its weaknesses to accomplish its mission?[10]

Organisational Registration

Once a voluntary development organisation is created then the question of providing a legal identity to it acquires significance. Pressures to provide legal identity emanate from diverse sources – the most common is the requirement of outside environment to relate with a legal entity. This requirement is imposed by donors, regulatory mechanisms, etc. The second pressure to provide a legal identity comes from the question of establishing an ongoing identity to the organisation, beyond the person of the founder(s).[11] Thus, an NGO can function as an unregistered organisation; however, legalisation provides, *inter alia*, the advantage of securing funds in a larger scale for expansion and greater thrust in the activities of the organisation.[12] Further, "providing a legal identity and ensuring

---

10. Bhose, Joel S.G.R., *op. cit.*, pp.43-44.
11. *Voluntary Development Organizations in India – A Study of History, Roles and Future Challenges*, Society for Participatory Research in Asia, New Delhi, November 1991, pp.67-68.
12. Stephen, T.S., *Guidelines for Voluntary Organisations*, PDC – Network, Bhubaneswar, 2003, p.21.

    On NGO registration Alan Fowler observes: "Choosing to gain social recognition by formal registration means accepting society's right to oversee that you do what you say you will. In other words, registration is accepting obligations of public accountability which society determines and regulates." See Fowler, Alan, *Striking a Balance: A Guide to Enhancing the Effectiveness of Non-Governmental Organisations in International Development*, *op. cit.*, p.22.

registration of a voluntary organisation makes it accountable to various organs of the state.... This accountability entails periodic reporting requirements in the form and manner prescribed by those organs and gives the rights to those organs to intervene in that voluntary organisation as they deem fit...."[13]

An NGO in the Indian context can be formed in the following four ways: trust, association or society, cooperative, and nonprofit company.[14]

Trust

A Trust is a body of which there can be three or more members as owners. This is a convenient and effective form of organisation when the unit is not unwieldy. It is easily manageable with the help of a few in key positions. A Trust thus constituted is registered under the Indian Trusts Act, 1882, and should be managed according to the terms of the said Act.[15] An NGO can also seek registration under the Charitable and Religious Trusts Act, 1920.[16]

Association or Society

This is a common form of voluntary organisation comprising seven or more members. It is governed by the Societies Registration Act, 1860. The NGO once formed can be registered at district, state or national level. An association form of NGO is

---

13. *Voluntary Development Organizations in India: A Study of History, Roles and Future Challenges, op. cit.*, p.68.
14. Stephen, T.S., *op. cit.*
15. *Ibid.*
    For details see *The Indian Trusts Act, 1882*.
16. *Report of the Steering Committee on Voluntary Sector for the Tenth Five-Year Plan (2002-2007)*, Planning Commission, Government of India, January 2002, pp.3-4.

better than any other form due to its inherent nature to ensure internal democracy and participation thereby attracting more funds and support.[17]

Cooperative

An organisation, if it suits its objectives, can be registered as a Cooperative Society under the Cooperative Societies Registration Act, 1962. The Registrar of Cooperative Societies of the State concerned provides model rules based on which organisation's own rules, regulations, among other things, should be based.[18]

Nonprofit Company

The Companies Act of 1956 under Section 25 provides for institutions that have no business character or profit motive to be registered under the Companies Act with a view to carrying out their objectives. NGOs established under this Act would be hardly many in view of the stringent of the provisions of the Act.[19]

Management Structure

In today's democratic world, participation is the buzzword guiding organisations. In theory and practice, NGOs are participatory in formation, as also in programme planning and functioning. Depending on management patterns or rules of management, NGOs are different from one another in structure. Each organisation tries to set its own rules of work that enables

---

17. Stephen, T.S., *op. cit.*
    For details see *The Societies Registration Act, 1860.*
18. Stephen, T.S., *op. cit.*, p.22.
19. *Ibid.*
    For details see *The Companies Act, 1956.*

them to plan and organise meetings, consultations, programmes, membership, and conduct business. Participatory management is the common thread of all NGOs.[20]

A standard NGO structure does have a **governing board, assembly** or **local advisory committee** on top of the organisational hierarchy at country, centre or central office level, under which the leadership can be located with delegated authority working with the organs of the NGO structure, viz., finance and administration. At field level the NGO management delivers its change agents with the support of finance and administration, technical wing and planning and learning to deal with the target communities, groups and individuals. Complementing the structure, NGOs have two major overlapping sets of systems: procedures, processes and recognised ways of working.[21]

An Indian NGO, in the course of being set up, devises a **memorandum of association** and **bye-laws.** The former gives details of NGO's organisational status, vision, mission and objective, and the latter details the management structures and systems and procedures of the organisation. The memorandum and bye-laws make up the constitution of the organisation. They are supposed to be observed by the constituents of the

---

20. Stephen, T.S., *op. cit.*, p.30.

    An NGO's structure depends also on its perception of what is the manageable level of its organisational complexity. There are three basic patterns to organise an NGO: by function *(where specialists in a function work together)*; by project, programme, product or location *(where specialists in several relevant functions work together to constitute multi-functional teams, each one much like a mini-NGO); and* as matrix organisation *(an economic and efficient, but complex combination of the above two patterns)*. For details see Chadha, Prem, Jagadananda and Lal, Gayatri, *op. cit.*, pp.91-103.

21. For details see Fowler, Alan, *Striking a Balance: A Guide to Enhancing the Effectiveness of Non-Governmental Organisations in International Development*, *op. cit.*, pp.58-61.

organisation in letter and spirit. Generally, an Indian NGO has the following three **management structures**[22], viz., General Body, Governing Body[23], Executive Staff and Chief Functionary.

General Body

The General Body, which consists of all the members of the organisation, is the apex body vested with the basic powers pertaining to the organisation, and is an organ of high significance. Decisions are taken on the basis of voting by majority, after full discussion in the meetings of the General Body. The strength of the General Body varies according to the size of the organisation. It mainly deals with broad policy issues, periodic election of its members and also performance evaluation of the organisation.

The General Body has the following functions: election of office bearers of the organisation; delegation of the management power to the Governing Body; passing of resolutions on important matters; approval of the annual reports and the audited statement of accounts; approval of action plan and budget; consideration of the resolutions passed by the Governing Body and approval of the same on satisfaction; effecting amendments to the constitution of the organisation where necessary; deciding dissolution or

22. Stephen, T.S., *op. cit.*, pp.30-31.

The memorandum contains the aims and objectives of the organisation and the bye-laws consist of the articles of association or the rules and regulations of the organisation concerned. While forming such an organisation, it is important to clearly delineate the power structure or the hierarchy within the organisation, pinpointing the control points therein, and specifying the powers, duties and responsibilities of members and office bearers concerned. *Ibid.*

23. Also called the **Managing Committee.**

termination of the organisation and settlement of its assets and liabilities.[24]

Governing Body

Governing Body comprises members elected from the General Body along with the office bearers. The tenure of the Governing Body is decided during formation of the organisation in the bye-laws. It constitutes the leadership or the real *management* of the organisation. Its membership varies according to the size of the General Body. The Governing Body is answerable only to the General Body. All major decisions taken by the Governing Body have to be approved in the annual General Body meeting of the organisation. Powers of the members of the Governing Body are equal and hence decisions are taken by a majority vote where these are not based on consensus. The following are the main functions of the Governing Body: appointment of the Chief Functionary and Executive Staff; financial management, (i.e., fund raising, fund utilisation, accounts *et al*); approving of the programme organised by the staff; passing resolutions on urgent matters; attending to legal matters; acting as the guarantor for projects supported by funding agencies.[25]

---

24. Stephen, T.S., *op. cit.*, pp.31-32.

    The General Body meets at least once a year. Notice should be given by the Secretary or Convener at least three weeks before the scheduled date of the meeting or as per the organisational bye-laws. The General Body meeting gives an opportunity to its members for a free discussion on the affairs of the organisation, its functioning, and suggests improvements where applicable. These meetings are vital for internal democracy of the organisation as also participatory functioning within it. *Ibid.*, p.32.

25. *Ibid.*, pp.32-33.

    Quality of leadership and governance is important to NGO's success. To ensure and sustain high quality of leadership and governance, it is essential that leadership development is seen and carried out as an ongoing process, resulting in the NGO having competent leaders

Executive Staff and Chief Functionary

The exercise of powers of the Governing Body is entrusted to the Chief Functionary and the Executive Staff. In other words, to implement its programmes a voluntary organisation depends on its Executive Staff. Proper coordination between the Governing Body and the Executive Staff is crucial for the success of an NGO. The Chief Functionary, who is the full-time administrator of the organisation, appoints the staff with the approval of the Governing Body. Executive Staff comprises of **administrative staff** (who deal with office management) and **programme** or **field staff** that include *Coordinators*, *Supervisors*, *Animators* or *Facilitators* and *Volunteers* (in charge of project implementation).[26]

The Chief Functionary is responsible for all his/her acts of commission and omission and answerable to the Governing

---

at all levels. The leadership must energize and motivate its members. It also requires sharp behavioral skills, sound understanding of the environment and the will to focus on purposes. For details on leadership need in NGO, see Chadha, Prem, Jagadananda and Lal, Gayatri, *op. cit.*, pp. 122-133.

26. Stephen, T.S., *op. cit.*, pp.36-44.

The Animators or Facilitators are the link between the people and the organisation. They are responsible for programme implementation in their respective areas. They are given training both in the field and at the center about survey guidelines, awareness creation, motivation, skill of organizing people, etc. The Animators are answerable directly to the Supervisor of the concerned area. Most of the Animators are appointed part-time on a nominal honorarium. Supervisors are appointed to organise and supervise the programme implementation in a particular area comprising several villages. Generally, five to ten Animators work under one Supervisor. They are trained in the managerial skill and properly informed of programme strategies. They report to the Coordinator. Every programme has a Coordinator, each responsible for monitoring and reporting the progress of the programme to the Chief Functionary. *Ibid.*, pp.48-49.

Body of which he or she is an ex-officio member. The Governing Body delegates its executive powers to the Chief Functionary to direct and manage the organisation as per the terms of the memorandum and bye-laws. His or her term of office is fixed by the Governing Body. As the chief executive of the organisation, the Chief Functionary has the following roles: provide direction and inspiration to the staff; select, train and motivate the staff; raise funds and get financial support; prepare projects, budgets and reports; represent the organisation at various forums; maintain proper relation with the public, government, support agencies and fellow NGOs; organise meetings of General Body, Governing Body, Staff, etc.; get the accounts audited and attend the work relating thereto; supervise the projects and programmes of the organisation.[27]

It is a common practice to have some eminent persons from public life as **advisors** of the organisation.[28] Their function is to suggest for organisational improvement and taking up new initiatives. With the rapid growth of organisations both in number and size, the role of such advisors or consultants has become more important and crucial. A consultant is not a member of the organisation, but an expert invited to provide professional advice in solving problems and improving performance.[29]

---

27. *Ibid.*, p.51.
28. Some NGOs prefer to have **Advisory Council** with subject experts.
29. Stephen, T.S. *op. cit.*

4

NGOs: Functions

Development does not start with goods: it starts with people and their education, organisation, and discipline. The alleviation of poverty depends primarily on the removal of these three deficiencies.

– *E.F. Schumacher*

Nature of NGO Functions

Both individualism and statism, two major political ideologies in the modern world, have failed to create a meaningful relationship between the individual and the state. Either ideology may lead to anomie and alienation – the one because society has no place, the other because it becomes overbearing and all-pervasive. NGOs as **mediating institutions**[1] resolve the situation for the individual. These institutions are not so large that individuals cannot identify with them, nor have any

1. Such mediating institutions can take a multitude of forms, for example, residential communities, workplaces, schools, churches, ethnic or cultural communities, charities, political groups, kinship networks – indeed any form of collectivity in which individual members can directly participate. See Moore, David B. and Schmitz, Gerald J., "Can We Define the Voluntary Sector?" (Eds.) by Tony F. Marshall, *Debating Development Discourse (Institutional and Popular Perspectives)*, Macmillan Press Ltd., 1995, p.58.

meaningful and effective involvement in them. They, by themselves, link the individual to the nation-state. While the private sector allows room for individualism, and the statutory sector for those basic services that should be available to all members of society, the voluntary sector serves individuals to share in, and contribute to, a meaningful association with the cultural stock of the nation, in addition to the material and psychological commonweal and political action. Gladstone called it **'welfare pluralism'**.[2]

NGOs are grassroots organisations which work with an **action-research methodology.**[3] 'Participatory development' involves the beneficiaries as partners and as co-workers in action and in research. Although participation is more and more an accepted philosophy, projects lack in popular participation. Development has mostly left the poorest people behind. The 'trickle-down' from growth theories has produced mainly the poverty of urban slums. Faced with such a situation, **leaders worldwide have come to see the grassroots development work of the voluntary agencies as a possible way out, even though it may not lead to wealth, but to Gandhian levels of self-sufficiency, basic needs and rural dignity.**[4]

E.F. Schumacher, who was the philosopher of the western NGO movement, is famous for his book *Small is Beautiful,* writes about NGO functions thus: "Development does not start with goods: it starts with people and their education,

---

2. *Ibid.*, pp.57-58.
3. The **action-research methodology** asks the practitioner never to carry out an action without studying its effects, but always carry out the research taking the target people in question, so that it leads to greater impact for the actions.
4. Poulton, Robin and Harris, Michael (Eds.), "On Theories and Strategies" by Robin Poulton, *Putting People First: Voluntary Organisations and Third World Development*, Macmillan, 1988, p.30.

organization, and discipline. If the primary causes of poverty are deficiencies in those three respects, then the alleviation of poverty depends primarily on the removal of these three deficiencies. Here lies the reason why development cannot be an act of creation, why it cannot be ordered, bought, comprehensively planned: why it requires a process of evolution." **There is, thus, the justification for long-term participatory development (and failure of the project cycle[5]), which only the institutions of voluntary nature can make happen.**[6]

The role of the NGOs is not to carry out development by themselves. **The role is to add 'participation' to the development equation. Participation means working with all the people.**[7] "NGOs cannot provide a national extension service, or a national policy for sectoral development. That is the job of the government. NGOs cannot build a dam to control irrigation water or to provide electricity. Such huge investments are decided by the government. Where NGOs can play a role, is in communication with the farmers. To help them to understand what will change, to help them to reorganise their methods of production, to help them to obtain necessary inputs, to help them to resist exploitation under the new regime is a role which the voluntary agencies are uniquely qualified to play."[8]

---

5. "The weakest part of the voluntary movement is the '**salt and pepper syndrome**;' what the French call ***saupoudrage.*** If assistance is scattered like salt and pepper on a plate of food, then it achieves very little. To be effective, aid must be professional, concentrated, and long-term. As long as donors continue to plan *project,* they will continue to break up the development process." *Ibid.*, p.23.
6. *Ibid.*, p.31.
7. *Ibid.*

   The influence of Gandhi has led the participatory approach to development towards community development. The following equation explains the position well: **Basic needs + Participatory development = Community development (over a period of 25 years).** *Ibid.*
8. *Ibid.*, p.25.

The Brazilian author, Paulo Freire,[9] through his writings on **conscientisation,**[10] had a great impact on NGOs (particularly in Latin America). **Such NGOs are building up the structures which will allow peasants not only to claim, but to gain a share of power.**[11]

Basic needs approach can broadly be summarised under ecological balance, better food and quality of life. It is desirable that all the components of the basic needs should reach the people. **The voluntary agencies are effective in applying the basic needs approach to poverty alleviation.**[12]

Since the Second World War, the international bodies have promoted a style of development that has often been insensitive to the needs of ordinary people and to the environment. Similarly, southern governments have typically pursued policies that serve the elite at the expense of the poor. There is now near-universal recognition that poverty alleviation, eradication of hunger, protecting the environment, grassroots development and safeguarding the poor from the debt crisis are priorities. But these are areas in which the official agencies have limited experience or encounter tremendous operational difficulties and as a result they are actively seeking the collaboration of both northern and southern NGOs. **The voluntary organisations often work in the areas of greatest poverty, have direct relationships with the communities of poor**

---

9. He was considered subversive and dangerous by many governments. See Poulton, Robin and Harris, Michael (Eds.), *op. cit.*, p.31.
10. For details on conscientisation, see (a) Freire, P., *Conscientisation and Liberation,* Institute of Cultural Action, 1973; (b) Freire, P., *By Learning They Can Teach*, University of Dar Es Salam, Dar Es Salam, 1971; (c) Freire, P., *Pedagogy of the Oppressed,* Penguin, Harmondsworth, 1972.
11. Poulton, Robin and Harris, Michael (Eds.), *op. cit.*, p.31.
12. *Ibid.*, pp.31-32.

people and have considerable experience of tackling environmental problems.[13]

Voluntary organisations perform particularly three important roles in a democracy. In their **political roles**, they supplement political parties as flexible mechanisms through which citizens define and articulate a broad range of interests, meet local needs, and make demands on the government. In their **educational roles**, they provide training grounds for democratic citizenship, develop the political skills of their members, recruit new political leaders, stimulate political participation, and educate the larger public on a wide variety of public interest issues. In their **watchdog roles** they serve, along with the press, as checks on "... the relentless tendency of the state to centralise its power and to evade civic accountability and control."[14]

---

13. Clark, John, *Democratizing Development: The Role of Voluntary Organizations*, Kumarian Press, 1991, p.5.

    An important new role envisioned for many NGOs today stems from the widespread view that NGOs enjoy closer relationships with their rural constituents and, as a result, are more likely to engender their trust and participation than do government agencies. See Riley, John M., *Stakeholders in Rural Development: Critical Collaboration in State-NGO Partnerships*, Sage Publications, New Delhi, Thousand Oaks, London, 2002, p.78.

14. Korten, David C., *Getting to the 21st Century: Voluntary Action and the Global Agenda*, Kumarian Press, 1990, p.99.

    A somewhat critical view on the subject was expressed by Biggs and Neame. They said that the idea that NGOs can create civil society and democracy relies on a simplistic notion that these are goals that can be attained through programmes and projects, rather than through fundamental processes of societal and political change. For details see, Edwards, Michael and Hulme, David (Eds.) "Negotiating Room to Maneuver: Reflections Concerning NGO Autonomy and Accountability within the New Policy Agenda" by Biggs, Stephen D. and Neame, Arthur D. *Beyond the Magic Bullet: NGO Performance and Accountability in the Post-Cold War World*, Kumarian Press, West Hartfort CT, 1996, pp.40-52.

New concerns came to the fore in 1980s, such as gender and environment, with social forestry and soil conservation prominent among environmental concerns. The 1990s have witnessed yet more changes in the nature of NGO activities. Work in the areas of gender and environment has been widened and in many ways integrated under the umbrella of '**sustainable development**'. Additionally, some NGOs have focused their efforts in initiatives aimed at strengthening the power and influence of different (poorer) groups in civil society, and in a range of projects and programmes striving to build up the capacity of local organisations.[15]

It is beyond any doubt that the mainstay of **NGOs' contribution to development is not financial, but organisational.** The organisational capacity that comes of life through NGOs represents its fundamental strategic resource and crucial contribution. The essence of the NGO approach is not to induce development financially, but to mobilise people into organised structures of voluntary group action for self-reliance and self-development. NGOs themselves are one expression of such voluntarism incorporated into organised structures. In turn, NGOs mobilise voluntarism further, thus amplifying the social energy put in the service of people's self-government.[16]

The first and foremost NGO emphasis is on purposively organising people for reaching their common objectives. This way, NGOs are '**putting people first**' in their work as a methodology and as a goal. They organise people to make better use of their own local productive resources, to create new resources

---

15. Riddel, Roger and Robinson, Mark, *Non-Governmental Organizations and Rural Poverty Alleviation,* Overseas Development Institute, London, Clarendon Press, Oxford, 1995, p.35.
16. Cernea, Michael M., *40, World Bank Discussion Papers: Non-governmental Organizations and Local Development,* The World Bank, Washington D.C., 1988, p.7.

and services, to promote equity and alleviate poverty, to influence government actions towards these same objectives and to establish new institutional frameworks that will sustain people-centered or actor-centered development.[17]

David Korten speaks of four generations of NGO functions. **First generation** functions or strategies grew out of a long history of international voluntary action aimed at assisting the victims of wars and natural disasters, and providing welfare services to the poor. Religious groups commonly have been at the forefront of these efforts. **Second generation** functions or strategies focus the energies of NGOs on developing the capacities of the people to better meet their own needs through self-reliant local action. Because of their attention to sustainability, true second generation strategies are developmental in concept, and are often referred to as community development strategies. **Third generation** functions or strategies look beyond the individual community and seek changes in specific policies and institutions at local, national and global levels. **Fourth generation** functions or strategies look beyond focused initiatives aimed at changing specific policies and institutional sub-systems. Their goal is to energise a critical mass of independent, decentralised initiative in support of a social vision.[18]

John Clark refers to the shift in the types of activities conducted by NGOs as they progress through this evolution as a progression, from a supply-side approach to local development (in which organisations focus on implementing services or projects) to a demand-side orientation. In the demand-side approach, he says, an **NGO's purpose is to help communities**

17. *Ibid.*, pp.7-8.
18. For details see Korten, David C., *op. cit.*, Kumarian Press, 1990 pp.115-126.

articulate their preferences and concerns so as to become active participants in the development process.[19]

Najam conceptualised NGOs as **policy entrepreneurs** whose principal function is advocacy for social change.[20]

According to Anil Bhatt, modern voluntarism aims at achieving **development and social justice.** Modern voluntarism strives to change the social, economic and political position of the poor, the deprived, the oppressed, and the weak. In the final analysis, therefore, it aims at the redistribution of power, wealth, and status.[21]

Role of NGOs Envisaged by Government

Though association with the people's institution had been emphasised since the First Five-Year Plan in India, for the first

---

19. For details see Clark, John, "The State, Popular Participation and the Voluntary Sector", *World Development*, 23(4), 1995, pp.593-601.
20. Edwards, Michael and Fowler, Alan (Eds.), "Strategy and Structure in Managing Global Associations", by Young, Dennis R., Koenig, Bonnie L., Najam, Adil and Fisher, Julie, *The Earthscan Reader on NGO Management*, Earthscan, 2003, p.150.

    "...voluntary organisations can play a dynamic role in empowering the poor by fostering greater mobilization and awareness-generation among them.... NGOs can help to motivate, organise and conscientise the poor, and provide them with an interface with bureaucracy and elected body." See for details Prasad, Kamta and Madaan, Davinder K. (Eds.), "Rural Development and the Role of NGOs in India" by P. Jagadish Gandhi, *NGOs and Socio-Economic Development Opportunities*, Deep and Deep Publications Pvt. Ltd., New Delhi, 2001, pp.33-34.
21. For details see Heyzer, Noeleen, Riker, James V. and Quizone, Antonio B. (Eds.), "Asian NGOs in Development: Their Role and Impact" by Bhatt, Anil, *Government NGO Relations in Asia: Prospects and Challenges for People Centred Development*, Kuala Lumpur, Asian and Pacific Development Centre, 1985, Chapter 4.

time the **Sixth Plan** document (1980-85) of the Government of India, indicated in detail the following role for NGOs in India:[22]

> Optimal utilisation and development of renewable source of energy, including forestry, family welfare, health and nutrition, education; 'health for all' programmes; water management and soil conservation; social welfare programmes for weaker sections; implementation of minimum needs programme; disaster preparedness and management; promotion of ecology and tribal development; environmental protection and education.

The **Seventh Plan** (1985-90) envisaged a greater role for NGOs in the implementation of development plans. They are as under:[23]

> Supplement government effort so as to offer the rural poor choices and alternatives; voluntary agency to adopt simple, innovative, flexible and inexpensive means with its limited resources to reach a large number with fewer overheads and with greater community participation; activate the delivery system and to make it effective at the village level to respond to the felt needs of the poorest of the poor; disseminate information, make communities as self-reliant as possible, to show how village and indigenous resources could be used, how human resources, rural skill and local knowledge grossly underutilised at present could be used for their own development, demystify technology and bring it in a simple form to the rural poor; train a cadre of grass-roots workers who believe in professionalising voluntarism; mobilise financial resources from within the community with a view to making communities stand on their own feet; mobilise and organise the poor and generate awareness to demand quality services and impose a community system of accountability on the performance of village level government functionaries.

---

22. Bava, Noorjahan, (Ed.), *Non-Governmental Organisations in Development: Theory and Practice*, Kanishka Publishers and Distributors, 1997, p.128.
23. *Ibid.*, pp.132-133.

In the **Eighth Plan** Document, due emphasis was given on building up people's institutions. It was admitted that a lot in the areas of education (especially literacy), health, family planning, land improvement, efficient land use, minor irrigation, watershed management, recovery of wastelands, afforestation, animal husbandry, dairy, fisheries and sericulture, etc. could be achieved by creating people's institutions accountable to the community. Therefore, the **focus of attention was on developing multiple institutional options for improving the delivery systems by using the vast potential of the voluntary sector.**[24]

In the **Ninth Plan**, it was admitted that private initiative, whether individual, collective or community based, forms the essence of the development strategy articulated in the Plan and efforts to be made to remove disadvantages which had prevented some segment of society in participating effectively in the development process. Keeping up with this line of thinking, **promoting and developing people's participatory bodies was one of the objectives of the Ninth Plan.** The mid-term review of the Plan suggested that initiatives by local bodies, NGOs and women needed to be encouraged, to resolve the problems relating to balanced growth of different regions of India and building institutions for maximising development outcomes and effectiveness and efficiency of public service delivery.[25]

The theme of encouragement to voluntary sector continued in the Approach Paper to the **Tenth Plan** and was reflected in the following words: "In view of the continued importance of public action in our development process, increasing the efficiency of public interventions must also take high priority." The minimum agenda proposed in the Approach Paper has

24. *Report of the Steering Committee on Voluntary Sector for the Tenth Five-Year Plan (2002-2007)*, Planning Commission, Government of India, January 2002, pp.8-10.

25. *Ibid.*

recognised voluntary sector by according greater decentralisation to Panchayati Raj Institutions and other people's organisations as one of the items for the Tenth Plan.[26]

Efforts of the Government of India from First to Tenth Five-Year Plan in promoting collaboration with the voluntary sector are given in **Annexure I** in greater detail.

26. *Ibid.*

5

NGOs: Accountability and Autonomy

Give a man a fish and you feed him for today – teach him how to fish and he feeds himself and his family for the rest of their lives.

– Saying of Lao Tse and popularised by Ritchie Caider

Accountability

Organisations exist and operate within a complex and dynamic web of social, economic, cultural and political surroundings. It is impossible for NGOs to operate in complete isolation. One factor important for any organisation intended to play an important role in shaping the nature of society and individuals is accountability.[1] Edwards and Hulme defines it as the 'means' by which individuals and organisations report to a recognised authority (or authorities) and are held responsible for their actions.[2]

---

1. Riley, John M., *Stakeholders in Rural Development: Critical Collaboration in State-NGO Partnerships*, Sage Publications, New Delhi, Thousand Oaks, London, 2002, pp.79-80.
2. Edwards, Michael and Hulme, David (Eds.), *Beyond the Magic Bullet: NGO Performance and Accountability in the Post-Cold War World*, Kumarian Press, West Hartford CT, 1996, p.8.

The term 'NGO accountability' has many meanings. It includes accountability of an NGO to grassroots constituents, to donors for resource use, and "strategic accountability for outcomes that NGOs have on the wider environment."[3] It appears that the more successful NGOs are in achieving multiple accountability, the less independent they become. Yet more areas of accountability may also provide them with greater room to manoeuvre.[4]

Autonomy

Organisational autonomy is defined as **the freedom to make decisions with the optimal degree of discretion.** This has an interesting twist in the Third World context related to accountability. Grassroots organisations need to be accountable to their members, rather than be autonomous from them. By the same token, a grassroots support organisation's autonomy from grassroots organisations would mean that the former is not accountable. Networks also need to be accountable to their member organisations while preserving their autonomy from donors and governments. **The meaning of autonomy, therefore, should be confined to what might be called upward relationships.** Grassroots organisations and their networks should be autonomous from grassroots support organisations, donors, and governments; grassroots support organisations and their networks should be autonomous from governments and donors.[5]

---

3. *Ibid.*
4. Edwards, Michael and Hulme, David (Eds.), "Negotiating Room to Maneuver: Reflections Concerning NGO Autonomy and Accountability within the New Policy Agenda" by Biggs, Stephen D. and Neame, Arthur D., *Beyond the Magic Bullet: NGO Performance and Accountability in the Post-Cold War World*, Kumarian Press, West Hartfort CT, 1996, pp.48-49.
5. Fisher, Julie, *Nongovernments: Political Development of the Third World*, Kumarian Press, 1998, pp.77-78.

Accountability vs. Autonomy

Nelson observes that NGOs' accountability is often related to issues of scale. Most major donor projects involving NGOs enlist them to do community organising or service delivery as part of an effort to extend benefits into poor or remote rural areas where a government has little presence or credibility. But **participating in a large-scale donor project can lead to a shift in an NGO's emphasis from community based to donor-initiated activities, thereby compromising its own autonomy.** For international NGOs, whose links to local groups in the Third World are inherently difficult, forming close programme associations with national and international donors can create tensions between donors and partners.[6]

Larry Minear warns that 'P' in PVO could soon be taken to mean not private but public or parastatal. NGOs' responsiveness to increasingly frequent cooperative initiatives by major donors may threaten NGOs' reliance on local input in identifying projects, and compromise their ability to speak openly about problems in development assistance or foreign policy.[7] Planning and reporting requirements and the scale of donor programmes compel small NGO operations to become centred on bureaucratic and official procedures, rather than the dynamics of grassroots initiative and critique.[8]

According to Clark, official funding of NGOs may be increasing but it is not possible to decipher from the figures how

---

6. Nelson, Paul J., *The World Bank and Non-Governmental Organizations: The Limits of Apolitical Development*, Macmillan Press Ltd. and St. Martin's Press, Inc., New York, 1995, pp.48-49.
7. *Ibid.*, p.50.
8. Bebbington, Anthony and Farrington, John, "Governments, NGOs and Agricultural Development: Perspective on Changing Inter-Organizational Relationships", *Journal of Development Studies*, 29(2), 1993, pp.207-208.

much is channelled for purposes designed freely by the NGOs. Public service contractors will often tailor their projects to suit the official aid agencies. The carry-over effect of these trends is that local development efforts in the Third World are being distorted towards the interpretation of the non-radical NGOs. The immense funding of these spawns local partners anxious to meet the job descriptions defined by the funders, who in turn draft those job descriptions mindful of the interests of their major donors. This amounts to a neat reversal of bottom-up ideas of development and can be disruptive. Non-radical NGOs are increasingly seen as preferred partners by many major official aid agencies and Southern governments. In response, some radical NGOs have advocated drawing up an NGO Charter or Code of Conduct to define the responsibilities of all NGOs.[9]

It is difficult to reconcile the concept of accountability with autonomy. As ideal types, they are completely incompatible ideas. Practically, though, absolute autonomy is an impossibility as organisations cannot perform public activities in an operational vacuum. At the other extreme, complete accountability to all involved individuals and organisations would make it impossible for an NGO to conform to all outside demands. The extremes of complete autonomy and rigid accountability must be reconciled, if NGOs are to be able to maintain their unique organisational characteristics, while at the same time satisfying the demand of others.[10]

Keys to Autonomy

Julie Fisher gives seven keys to NGO autonomy. First is a clear, self-conscious **organisational commitment to autonomy**. The

---

9. Clark, John, *Democratizing Development: The Role of Voluntary Organizations*, Kumarian Press, 1991, pp.38-39.
10. Riley, John M., *op. cit.*, p.81.

second key is **diversified financial support** that enables NGOs to be independent of any single donor, including the government. The third is **strong grassroots ties.** Grassroots support organisations' autonomy is also enhanced by three related kinds of knowledge – **technical expertise, managerial excellence, and strategic knowledge about development**, which is needed for a successful demonstration project. They constitute fourth, fifth and sixth keys respectively to NGO autonomy. Finally, the seventh key to autonomy is **staff experience in training government professionals**, which enhances the self-confidence and autonomy of GRSOs while propelling them towards continuing active contacts with governments.[11]

11. Fisher, Julie, *op. cit.*, 1998, p.78.

6

NGOs: Relationships

Almost no government is so bad that it resolutely refuses to help the poor.

– John Clark

NGO-Government Relationship

Economic theories of the nonprofit sector suggest several different ways of understanding the relationship between government and not-for-profit organisations. Different strands of theory support the alternative views that nonprofit organisations operate independently as **supplements** to the government, work as **complements** to the government in a partnership relationship, or are engaged in an **adversarial** relationship of mutual accountability with the government. In the supplementary model, nonprofit organisations are viewed as fulfilling the demand for public goods left unsatisfied by the government. In the complementary view, they are seen as partners to the government, helping to carry out the delivery of public goods largely financed by the government. Nonprofit bodies in their adversarial role, prod the government to make changes in public policy and to maintain accountability to the public; reciprocally, the government attempts to influence the behaviour of nonprofit organisations by regulating its services and responding to its advocacy initiatives as well.[1] In a similar way, Clark has to say that an NGO can oppose the State, complement it, or reform it, but cannot ignore it.[2]

NGO Strategies for NGO-Government Relationship

Julie Fisher speaks of three strategies: **political isolation, political advocacy**, and **cooperation with government**, which NGOs and their networks use to achieve the twin challenges of empowerment and development through their contacts with governments.[3]

Political Isolation

Both GROs and GRSOs may consciously decide to steer clear of the state for some time, build a mass base, strengthen independent-sector networks; and develop alternative approaches to development that can influence policy over the long run. Isolation is particularly suited to repressive contexts.[4]

Political Advocacy

Political advocacy is also based on a refusal to be co-opted or controlled, but involves direct communication with the

---

1. Young, Dennis R., "Alternative Models of Government Nonprofit Sector Relations: Theoretical and International Perspectives", *Nonprofit and Voluntary Sector Quarterly,* Vol.29, No.1, A Publication of Arnova, Sage Publications, Inc, March 2000, pp.149-153.
2. Clark, John, *Democratizing Development: The Role of Voluntary Organizations*, Kumarian Press, 1991, pp.65-66.

   The NGO would position itself is not so much as a co-producer but as a co-director of these services, not taking responsibility for actual service delivery, but helping to strengthen the existing systems. These approaches are very different in style but all can be effective. Even 'bad' governments have 'good' departments with which NGOs can work. **Almost no government is so bad that it resolutely refuses to help the poor.** *Ibid.*
3. For details see Fisher, Julie, *op. cit.*, pp.108-122.
4. *Ibid.*

government about policy. Advocacy may involve everything from quiet negotiations on limited organisational objectives to mass protests on major issues.[5]

Cooperation with Government

Cooperation with government at the project level is far more common, whether initiated by NGOs or by governments. Cooperative project strategies include everything from parallel cooperation to full field collaboration. Cooperative strategies often coexist with advocacy within any given NGO.[6]

State Response to NGOs

A look at governmental responses to the growth of NGOs reveals a wide range of reactions and policies. At the most

5. *Ibid.*

NGO advocates use many different advocacy techniques: friendly persuasion, 'acupuncture' (willingness of NGOs to take on the state while becoming permanently involved in the process of change through the state), legal and lobbying efforts, electoral politics, networking, and mass advocacy. Advocacy has probably had more impact on service delivery than on service redistribution, more impact on local environmental crises than on national policy, and more impact on strengthening civil society than on instituting top-down democratic reforms. *Ibid.*

6. *Ibid.*

Although some GRSOs oriented towards advocacy shun cooperation with the government, other GRSOs point out that if organisations with strong grassroots ties are reluctant to cooperate with the governments, less scrupulous organisations attracted to official funding are likely to evolve towards meeting the Indian government's 'People Sector' challenge by channelling funds made available under the government programs to the poor instead of relying on foreign funds. Although cooperation between NGOs and the governments may be less likely than advocacy to lead to top-down democratisation, habits of give-and-take with NGOs may increase tolerance for the autonomy of civil society. *Ibid.*

repressive end of the spectrum are the governments that are fearful of NGO activity; indeed, some political leaders assume that 'non-governmental' means 'anti-governmental'. More subtle forms of **repression against NGOs** have occurred as it has grown in power and influence.[7]

A second governmental approach has been to **ignore NGOs.** In the early 1970s until the mid-1980s, this was probably the most common governmental response. Ignoring NGOs is often less a deliberate policy than a symptom of the 'soft state',[8] incapable of carrying out any kind of coherent public policy. As NGOs have proliferated and become more politically active the governments have found it increasingly difficult to ignore them.[9]

A third general policy approach is **co-optation,** often caused by the tension between the need for more resources and the desire to control NGOs. Such close partnerships may be mutually beneficial. The state may also try to co-opt GROs, sometimes by creating its own local organisations.[10]

A fourth general policy approach is for the state to **take advantage** of but not necessarily attempt to control NGOs or to learn from them.[11]

---

7. *Ibid.*, pp.40-41.

   Subtle harassment may not represent a government-wide policy; indeed, it is often limited to particular ministries or departments. On the plus side, such schizophrenic policies can show up within extremely repressive regimes. *Ibid.*
8. in Gunnar Myrdal's language.
9. Fisher, Julie, *op. cit.*, pp.40-41.
10. *Ibid.*, p.42.

    Attempts to control GRSOs may take the form of subtle bribery, as in Tamil Nadu, where the social welfare board regularly gives small grants to GRSOs for 'furnishings.' *Ibid.*
11. *Ibid.*

A fifth general government policy is for the state and NGOs to cooperate and learn from each other in an **autonomous partnership**, which may be either *ad hoc* in nature or system-wide. Cooperation is sometimes the result of other kinds of NGO-government contacts.[12]

NGO-Funder Relationship
Extent of Fund Support for NGOs

A key factor that has contributed to the enhanced recognition given to the NGO movement is the increased role played by international and national NGOs in raising private funds for development and channelling them to developing countries. "Mounting public support in the rich countries of the North has given their NGOs a much stronger financial base. Northern NGOs collectively now transfer to the South more than the World Bank group does."[13]

"NGOs are generally seen as worthy and efficient but negligible on the scale of development needs. This may be true individually, but collectively NGOs now constitute one of the major channels of finance from North to South."[14] Over the period 1970-85, NGOs' yearly disbursements for development

---

Obviously, there are financial reasons for this. As Bebbington and Farrington point out, "participation is being grudgingly offered because [governments] can no longer finance patronage." Another reason for passive acceptance of NGOs is the need to enhance government legitimacy. Still another reason that governments may take advantage of NGOs is for military or security purposes. GRSOs generally lack a parochial ideology, so their resources are less likely than those of the government to be the target of ethnic and tribal rivalries. The last reason is that governments may be unable to make major reforms without NGO support. *Ibid.*

12. *Ibid.*
13. Cernea, Michael M., *40, World Bank Discussion Papers–Nongovernmental Organizations and Local Development*, The World Bank, Washington D.C., 1988, p.3.
14. Clark, John, *op. cit.*, p.44.

in the Third World increased from an estimated US$0.9 billion in 1970 to US$1.4 billion in 1975, and to US$4 billion in 1985."[15] In 1989 they shifted US $6.4 billion to the South. In terms of **net transfers** – and in the age of debt crisis, when the cash flow of developing countries is all important, NGOs collectively contribute more than the World Bank.[16]

In an era of declining financial resources available for development purposes in most Third World countries, the incremental resources supplied by NGOs are particularly valuable. At present, over 2,200 NGOs mobilise financial and human resources in DCA member countries for projects they operate directly or in partnership with countless associations and groups in developing countries. At the same time, the major donor governments of OECD countries have allocated a fraction of their official development assistance (ODA) to NGOs for use in NGO-initiated activities. This fraction has increased eleven times between 1975 and 1985, and to a total of $1.1 billion. Even the private funds raised and used by NGOs came to represent in 1985 a full 10 per cent of the ODA funds provided by OECD countries.[17]

NGOs and World Bank

The World Bank began to develop its relation with NGOs more systematically in the early 1980s. In 1982, a World Bank-NGO committee was established, which provided a formal coordinating forum and a focal point for the Bank's dealings with NGOs. The multiple activities currently underway can be summed up under four main areas:[18] **operational** collaboration in projects and programs; **development education; policy dialogue** between the World Bank and NGOs, particularly on

15. Cernea, Michael M., *op. cit.*, p.7.
16. Clark, John, *op. cit.*, p.44.
17. Cernea, Michael M., *op. cit.*, pp.5-7.
18. *Ibid.*, pp.28-42.

poverty alleviation and environmental issues; and **public frameworks** for NGOs.

In defining the NGOs with which it seeks to collaborate, the World Bank's policy takes a broad, non-restrictive position:

> The Bank's policy recognizes the **nature** of NGOs as **private organisations that pursue activities to relieve suffering, promote the interest of the poor, protect the environment or undertake community development.** Production-related NGOs are seen as particularly relevant to the Bank's development objectives, and such grassroots organisations include: water users' societies, pastoral associations, consumer and credit cooperatives, farm equipment purchase and lease associations, tree-grower associations and other similar groups. Environmental and emergency relief NGOs are in turn relevant to the Bank's objectives regarding the environment, support for resettlement and reconstruction, etc.[19]

The policy guidelines state that, although the Bank's primary relationships are with governments, collaboration with NGOs can improve the effectiveness of many Bank-supported operations, particularly in terms of increasing the long-term sustainability of development initiatives and alleviating poverty.[20]

Indian NGOs and Funders

It is useful to understand the various types of agencies involved in providing funding to voluntary development organisations in India. Broadly speaking, there are four types of foreign funding institutions. The first type is **bilateral institutions.** Bilateral aid from agencies, departments and ministries of governments of the North to governments of the South is a long-standing phenomenon since the end of Second World War. A substantial

19. *Ibid.*, p.43.
20. *Ibid.*

portion of this aid goes to government agencies. A very small portion of this aid has been made available to voluntary development organisations. The second type of institutions is **multilateral institutions** – consisting primarily of the agencies of the UN system. Their support to voluntary development organisations in a country like India is also much smaller, largely because it has to be approved by the government and the bulk of it goes to government agencies. The third category of support comes from **solidarity groups**, trade unions and other related bodies in the countries of the North by way of raising resources from their members and citizens to support programmes by agencies of the South.[21]

In the fourth category are the **northern NGOs** playing a funding role for voluntary organisations in the South. Most of these are in Europe, USA, Canada, etc. Broadly speaking, under this category, **three sub-categories** can be formed. One is the support from **church groups**. The second sub-category comprises **secular NGOs** in countries of the North where they raise resources from the public as well as governments and provide support to voluntary development organisations outside. A third sub-category consists of **Foundations** which are predominantly a North American phenomenon engaged in philanthropy. Ford and Rockefeller Foundations are examples of this form of funding.[22]

By and large, the support to voluntary development organisations in India comes from the fourth category of agencies, i.e., northern NGOs, also called international NGOs.[23] They display

---

21. *Voluntary Development Organizations in India: A Study of History, Roles and Future Challenges,* Society for Participatory Research in Asia, New Delhi, November 1991, p.78.

22. *Ibid.*, pp.78-79.

23. *Ibid.*, p.79.

"The bulk of voluntary agency in India is funded by international NGOs." *Ibid.*, p.142.

a marked preference for projects which centre on community development, incorporating a range of sector components, among them agriculture, credit, health and education. At the same time, they also tend to support activities that are popular in their own countries: women and environmental development that were popular issues of 1980s, which impacted national NGOs while receiving aid to tailor their programmes accordingly. International NGOs work for the most part in collaboration with national NGOs, acting as a conduit for funds, and comparatively few are involved directly in project implementation.[24]

Funding mechanism in India falls into four categories. The first is where the donor operates exclusively through an **intermediary agency** which is responsible for identifying suitable projects, liaising with partners, and monitoring and evaluating their activities. The second type is the **consortia model** favoured by the churches, where donor agencies pool their funds, usually in the form of block grants, which are then distributed by an intermediary agency. The third approach is that favoured by Oxfam, Save the Children Fund, and NOVIB, all of which have **in-country offices,** staffed mainly by Indian nationals, forming part of the parent organisation and performing a role similar to that of an intermediary agency. A variant on this approach is where the funding agency assumes a more active role in project planning, implementation and evaluation through an in-country office.[25]

The fourth model does not involve an intermediary agency, and relations between **donor and recipient operate on a one-to-one basis.** Projects are submitted directly to the funding

---

24. Riddel, Roger and Robinson, Mark, *Non-Governmental Organizations and Rural Poverty Alleviation,* Overseas Development Institute, London, Clarendon Press, Oxford, 1995, p.142.
25. *Ibid.,* pp.142-143.

agency which processes the applications in its head office. The main form of contact with project partners is through periodic tours undertaken by desk officers of the agency concerned.[26]

Of late, official donors are more willing to channel a proportion of their bilateral aid funds through NGOs, usually in the form of co-financing to international NGOs. Some have explored the potential for direct funding of Indian NGOs, but the government has tended to discourage this. Moreover, official donors lack the staff resources to monitor small grants directly or to develop a sufficiently detailed knowledge of the voluntary sector, with the result that most prefer to channel funds through NGOs from their own country. Legislation governing the receipt of funds from abroad consists mainly of the Foreign Contributions Regulation Act (FCRA), 1976. It compels all organisations wishing to receive funds from abroad to register with the Home Ministry, to submit audited accounts on a half-yearly basis, and provide details of each individual contribution.[27]

Recent estimates suggest that the amount of foreign funds coming into India for use by NGOs each year is in the region of Rs. 9 billion. In quantitative terms, this is equivalent to approximately 20 per cent of official aid flows in 1991. When individual and corporate donations are added in, an annual income figure of Rs. 10 billion would seem a reasonable estimate of the total available resources, although this does not take into account unofficial payments or contributions in kind by project beneficiaries. This figure is double the government's annual expenditure on IRDP, and 10 per cent of its overall budget is meant for poverty alleviation and service provision. This indicates that the resources mobilised by NGOs are

26. *Ibid.*

27. *Ibid.*

important but essentially supplement to those provided by the government.[28]

NGO-NGO Relationship

Purpose of Networks and Their Impact

Why do voluntary organisations want to associate with each other? Historically, there seem to be three dominant reasons. The first reason is to **overcome isolation.** Second, the desire for association comes from the need to **influence macro level.** The third dominant reason for coming together is **protection of space,** identity, legitimacy and credibility.[29] "Since it has become nearly impossible in many countries for individuals to advance themselves, they have begun to organize collectively.... The linkages among NGOs, coupled with the computer revolution, provide enormously enhanced capabilities for implementing sustainable development..." and equality.[30]

---

28. Riddel, Roger and Robinson, Mark, *Non-Governmental Organizations and Rural Poverty Alleviation, op. cit.*, pp.139-140.

    As per Government of India records, during 1991-92 (15 months period) Indian voluntary agencies received Rs. 1,412.13 crore, which increased to Rs. 3,924.63 crore during 1999-2000. See *A Compendium of Partnership between Government and Voluntary Sector: All India Conference on the Role of the Voluntary Sector in National Development, 20th April, 2002 New Delhi,* Planning Commission, Government of India, New Delhi, Annexure IV, p.268.

29 *Voluntary Development Organizations in India: A Study of History, Roles and Future Challenges*, Society for Participatory Research in Asia, New Delhi, November 1991, p.61.

30. Fisher, Julie, *op. cit.*, p.10.

    To be sure, individual GROs and GRSOs can become sources of privilege and patronage for the few, yet the linkages among NGOs, coupled with the computer revolution, provide enormously enhanced capabilities for implementing sustainable development and for creating paths to change that may violate Robert Michels's 'iron law of oligarchy.' There is evidence that the link between 'human nature' and 'oligarchic behavior' is not always inevitable. *Ibid.*

According to Julie Fisher, **GROs while being active on their own get activated by GRSOs also.** Due to various reasons, such as combined deterioration of their environment, increasing level of poverty of the 1980s, and gradual liberation of women, both traditional, and newly created GROs in Asia, Africa and Latin America are organising regional networks among themselves.[31]

Regarding the benefits of the networks, she says that GRO networks help scale up impact of programmes carried out by GROs; they are more accountable to local people than any other development institution; and they are often in the forefront of understanding the connections between poverty and environmental degradation. Moreover, horizontal linkages between GROs seem to have an additive impact on both participation and equality.[32]

Networks at both the grassroots and grassroots support levels not only enhance the sustainability of individual organisations but also help address the difficult challenge of scaling out the reach of sustainable development. Given the spread of GRO and GRSO networks, it is obvious that hundreds of

---

NGDOs use organising as a tool to empower their constituents. Yet, they do not seem to have successfully organised themselves as a sector. **Organising and aligning sectoral initiatives can cause knowledge and perspectives to be shared, provide for mutual help to develop new capacities for action.** For details see Chadha, Prem, Jagadananda and Lal, Gayatri, *op. cit.*, p.21.

31. Fisher, Julie, *op. cit.*, p.6.
32. *Ibid.*, pp.6-7.

There is an enormous amount of development activity happening with and institution building occurring within GROs. There is no definite measure as to how much of outside technical assistance that GROs should receive and how much self-reliance they should maintain to preserve their original character. *Ibid.*

thousands of activists understand the need for an impact on wider systems.[33]

Types of Networks

Regional or horizontal GROs networks link local community organisations in three different ways. First are the **formal umbrella networks** that link individual GROs such as cooperatives, local development associations, and interest associations. Second are the **informal economic networks** tied together by barter arrangements that can widen local markets and build a vested interest in regional collaboration. Third are the **amorphous grassroots social movements** that increasingly focus on environmental concerns; they may or may not be based on individual GROs. In some cases, GRO networks become self-supporting and create GRSOs from below by hiring their own expertise.[34]

In addition to building linkages with GROs, **GRSOs are uniting with one another**, both formally and informally. Both formal and informal networks may be **multi-sectoral** or may focus more narrowly on **one development sector**. And they may be **regional** or **national** in geographic focus.[35]

Formal umbrella organisations of GRSOs usually have written constitutions or bylaws and represent GRSOs as a group

---

33. *Ibid.*, p.10.

A.K. Choudhury visualised NGOs as part of Global Movement towards global transformation. To achieve this he suggested that NGOs should act as part of network or coalitions to promote peoples' movements at national and international levels. See Prasad, Kamta and Madaan, Davinder K. (Eds.), "NGOs and Their Role in Poverty Alleviation" by Anil Kumar Choudhury, *NGOs and Socio-Economic Development Opportunities*, Deep and Deep Publications Pvt. Ltd., New Delhi, 2001, p.40.

34. *Ibid.*, p.6.
35. *Ibid.*, pp.7-8.

in negotiations with governments and international donors. Although they often assist their member organisations, formal networks are not generally involved in grassroots support. The availability of funding can also lead to competition instead of collaboration among GRSOs. **GRSOs in informal networks** are more likely than those in formal networks to interact with one another in the field, and they may provide grassroots support as a group. The two most common types of informal networks are **service networks** and **support movements**. Service networks may be large or small, but they are consistently homogeneous, involving mainly GRSOs. Service networks enable GRSOs to exchange and promote one another's professional capacities. Support movements, in contrast, are large, heterogeneous, often amorphous systems of communication that include GRSOs, universities, charities, GROs, and some individuals, such as journalists or professors interested in grassroots development.[36]

Structure of International Networks

A study conducted recently revealed three broad categories of organisational structure among international networks having different levels of merits and demerits to the member organisations. The three structures are: corporate partnerships, federations and membership associations.[37]

- *Corporate Partnerships:* A unified corporation executes centrally directed project work or contracts with autonomous regional, national or sub-national partner organisations to carry out particular assignments. Under corporate partnership arrangements, corporate partners

36. *Ibid.*, pp.8-10.
37. For details see Edwards, Michael, Fowler, Alan (Eds.), "Strategy and Structure in Managing Global Associations" by Young, Dennis R., Koenig, Bonnie L., Najam, Adil and Fisher, Julie, *The Earthscan Reader on NGO Management*, Earthscan, 2003, pp.169-173.

are not involved in governance of the international organisation.

- *Federations:* An international body oversees or collaborates with a group of affiliates at the regional or national levels, which have comprehensive responsibility for carrying out the work of the association within their domains. This category includes strong federations in which the international organisation has substantial authority and weak confederations in which the international organisation is subordinate to its affiliates. Under the federation model, affiliates play a strong role as board members in some organisations, but a much weaker role in others.
- *Membership Associations:* Individual or organisational members belong to a central association and govern its operations, and which may develop chapters at the regional, national or local levels to carry out association work particular to those domains. Membership associations may be highly inclusive or they may restrict the number and types of members they admit.

NGO-Civil Society Relationship

What is Civil Society?

Proliferation of NGOs throughout the world has spurred interest in civil society, what Michael Walzer called 'the space of un-coerced human association'. In Latin America during the 1970s, intellectuals who were reacting against Marxism as well as right-wing dictatorship began to write about *sociedad civil*. During the 1980s, the term *civil society* reappeared in the writings of central and eastern European dissidents as they tried to carve out an understanding of social process that could stand in opposition to the state, while being broader and more humane than the market. Some observers, building on classical political theory, include the for-profit as well as the nonprofit sectors in their definitions of civil society. While Antonio

Gramsci described civil society in terms of **autonomous institutions that may either support or challenge state power,** Victor Perez Diaz defined it as '**markets, associations, and a sphere of public debate**'.[38]

NGO-Civil Society Interaction

The voluntary organisation, as David Korten says, is an **instrument** through which citizen volunteers establish an identity and legal recognition for their collective endeavours. There are **many levels of citizenship: community citizen, national citizen** and **global citizen.** It is the global citizen on whom the transformation of civil society depends, and upon whose commitment to global responsibility the foundations of a peoples' development movement must be built.[39]

In the Third World, NGOs are only part of the independent sector. The tendency to equate civil society and NGOs limits our understanding of a broad process of interaction among different types of organisations. Voluntary organisations, just like governments, are capable of destroying the independent grassroots initiatives that constitute social capital. Yet what is undeniable is that **voluntary organisations are the vanguard of civil society** in most of the Third World, including in the transitional countries of Europe and the former Soviet Union.[40]

---

38. Fisher, Julie, *op. cit.*, p.11.

    Interest in the concept of civil society is not new. John Locke wrote about its role in protecting property rights. *Ibid.*

39. Korten, David C., *Getting to the 21st Century: Voluntary Action and the Global Agenda*, Kumarian Press, 1990, p.108.

    The voluntary organisation exists to project the social commitment of its citizen volunteers. *Ibid.*

40. Fisher, Julie, *op. cit.*, pp.12-13.

In the Third World, NGOs promote civil society in **six major ways. First**, the strength of civil society is roughly related to the sheer number of functioning intermediary organisations between the citizen and the state.[41] NGO proliferation has played a **second** more specific role in nurturing sustainable development and viable civil societies in the Third World.[42] A **third**, more targeted, role for NGOs is to promote political rights and civil liberties.[43] A **fourth** way in which NGOs strengthen civil society is by focusing on bottom-up democratisation.[44] The **fifth** vanguard role played by NGOs is to influence other voluntary organisations. **Sixth**, NGOs are at the crux of the relationship between the for-profit and nonprofit sectors of civil society.[45]

---

41. Within the independent sector, these include everything from strictly civic associations, such as athletic teams, to NGOs that are trying to develop their communities or promote social change. *Ibid.*, pp.13-16.
42. GRSOs that focus on microenterprise development are building a vested interest in their work among the members of GROs. Since vested interests usually help sustain *inequitable* institutions, creating vested interests among the poor may be an equally powerful way to promote the institutional sustainability not only of microenterprise and cooperatives but also of the village councils or women's group that support such income strategies on a local level. *Ibid.*
43. There are now an estimated 4,000 to 5,000 indigenous human rights organisations at the most political ends of the NGO spectrum in the Third World, ranging from national chapters of Amnesty International to professional associations of lawyers or journalists. According to Welch they now exist in most African countries, unlike the situation barely a decade ago. *Ibid.*
44. Churches in Africa are establishing community outreach activities, and hospitals in many parts of the world are setting up preventive health care clinics in neighboring villages. *Ibid.*
45. By focusing on microenterprise development, NGOs broaden the ownership of capital, a connection that has the potential to challenge governments, because the habits of participation and empowerment necessitated by creating a business of women's clubs who created their own microenterprises and became the first women to participate in meetings of village councils. *Ibid.*

The most exciting phenomenon in the NGO sector in 1970s and 1980s has been the birth, growth and maturing of grassroots organisations throughout much of the Third World. Some have emerged from self-help projects which sought sustainability by investing control in the people. Others are entirely indigenous, emerging as local people responded to local problems. They have come to revolutionise the thinking of progressive NGOs about development itself. The early notion that 'our projects will be more effective if the people understand them better and take charge of their implementation' has given way to realisation that 'our projects will *be* better if they are based on the people's own analysis of the problems they face and their solutions'.[46] The social development approach sees the poor not as beneficiaries but as the controllers of the development process itself. The people must *make* the theory. What

---

The conceptualisation of the role of NGOs in strengthening civil society has gained currency in the 1990s amongst some of the bilateral aid agencies and international funding NGOs. State and civil society both influence each other and are both required to complete the process of governance. The civil society should be seen as an institutional site apart from not only the State, but also markets. The role of NGOs should be seen as strengthening the civil society, individually and collectively, so that a balanced relationship between political parties, government agencies and judiciary is achieved. See for details Prasad, Kamta and Madaan, Davinder K. (Eds.), "NGOs and Their Role in Poverty Alleviation" by Anil Kumar Choudhury, *NGOs and Socio-Economic Development Opportunities*, *op. cit.*, p.41.

46. Fisher, Julie, *op. cit.*, p.17.

When Islamic extremists destroyed the civil society that was emerging in Sudan in the second half of 1980s, and the National Islamic Front regime made it hard to restore social, religious, political and economic institutions, it appeared as if strengthening of civil society through the activities of NGOs as a rule is doubtful. Yet **as the vanguard of civil society in the Third World in general, NGOs not only enlarge its available space but also help create and enlarge the political commons where the state and civil society interact.** *Ibid.*

is revolutionary is not the improved efficiency of projects but the **unleashing of new-found confidence** of the people which in the final analysis strengthens the civil society.[47]

The poor remain in poverty because their way out is blocked, partly by lack of resources and by ignorance, but also because they don't believe there is anything they can do about it. NGO's support for schemes devised and run by the poor have shown that the poor can indeed control assets effectively to combat poverty, and that they have, collectively, an ability to take action that radically alters their situation. NGOs which campaign for reforming, which demonstrate by example that women and the poor are creditworthy, and that trade to and from remoter regions can be profitable, are in practice truer exponents of the free market system than those who voice monetarist rhetoric. **This unique contribution of NGOs strengthens the civil society and builds more of the social capital.**[48]

---

47. Clark, John, *op. cit., p.89.*
48. *Ibid.* pp. 89-103.

7

Development: Concept

Development means dams and factories, roads and canals, bush-clearing, electrification, soil improvement, universities, secondary schools, sanitation, research and a multitude of other activities and achievements But above all, development means people.

– ***Leopold Laufer***

The concept of development gained currency after the World War II and has been defined by most economists, in the operational sense, as growth of the per capita gross national product (GNP). There has been considerable criticism of this approach to development in view of a large number of developing countries failing to achieve a satisfactory rate of growth of per capita GNP. A number of observers have concluded that this has been basically due to the insufficient attention given to social and political factors in planning.[1] Thus, there is a need to define 'development' all inclusively.

According to the *Concise Oxford Dictionary of Current English* 'development' means "a stage of growth and advance-

1. Galnoor, Itzhak, "Social Information for What", *The Annals of the American Academy of Political and Social Science*, January 1971, p.8.

ment" and "a full grown state".[2] In the present day world, it has been viewed as "growth, evolution, stage of inducement or progress"[3] and often referred to the process of change aiming at progress in all directions.[4] It has been conceived as a "multidimensional process involving major changes in social structures, popular attitudes and national institutions, as well as the acceleration of economic growth, the reduction of inequality and the eradication of absolute poverty".[5] Development, further, has been defined in terms of "progressive reduction and eventual elimination of malnutrition, disease, illiteracy, squalor, unemployment and inequalities".[6] In course of time, the goal of development has as such become the enrichment of the quality of life and its availabiliry to all sections of the population.[7] Development, in consequence, has been a multifaceted and multidimensional concept and it is, therefore, defined differently by different scholars.[8] No single definition can provide a precise meaning to the term 'development'. A combined view on

---

2. *The Concise Oxford Dictionary of Current English*, Ninth Edition, Oxford University Press, 1995, pp.369-370.
3. Mehta, S.R., *Sociological Development in Mauritius: A Study of Rural Modernisation of an Island Community*, Wiley Eastern Ltd., New Delhi, 1983, p.1.
4. Al-Salem, F.S.A., *The Ecological Dimensions of Development Administration with Particular Reference to the Social System Environment of Administrative Systems in Low-income Countries*, Associated Publishing House, New Delhi, 1977, p.4.
5. Todaro, Michael P., *Economic Development in the Third World*, Longman Inc., New York, 1983, p.70.
6. Haq, Mahbub ul, "Employment and Income Distribution in the 1970s: A New Perspective," *Pakistan Economic and Social Review*, June-December, 1971, p.6.
7. Lakshman, T.K. et al. (Eds.), "Some Neglected Factors in Integrated Rural Development" by V.K.R.V. Rao, *Rural Development in India – A Multidimensional Analysis*, Himalayan Publishing House, Bombay, 1984, p.1.
8. Al-Salem, F.S.A., *op. cit.*, p.4.

the concept extended by different scholars may convey greater clarity on the matter.[9] Professor Gerald E Caiden's point in the matter is pertinent:

> "Nobody really knows what the word development really stands for any more. Economists identify it with economic productivity; Sociologists with social change or social differentiation; political scientists with democratization, political capacity or expanded government; administrators with bureaucratization, optimum efficiency, performance or capacity to assume all burdens."[10]

Leopold Laufer has the following observations on the term 'development':

> Development "means dams and factories, roads and canals, bush-clearing, electrification, soil improvement, universities, secondary schools, sanitation, research and a multitude of other activities and achievements. But above all, development means people. The preparation and activation of people is the cause of economic and social development."[11]

Further, Rosenstein Rodan, a well-known expert on economic development, has emphasised that "national development objectives relate not only to a rate of growth, but also to income distribution and other social goals."[12] Development in the new perspective has been referred to as an overall process of

---

9. *Ibid.*
10. Caider, Gerald E., as quoted *Ibid.*
11. Laufer, Leopold, *Israel and the Developing Countries: New Approaches to Cooperation,* New York, Twentieth Century Fund, 1967, p.69.
12. Rosentein Rodan, "Criteria for Evaluation of National Development Effort", *Journal of Development Planning,* 1, 1969, p. 5.

    Hirschman suggests that absence of 'extended family,' 'challenge,' 'love of money' or 'attitudinal change,' considered as barriers to development could either be converted into assets for development or their elimination can be postponed in the development process. See Hirschman, Albert, "Obstacles to Development: A Classification and a

transforming men and societies leading to a social order in which every human being can achieve moral and material well-being.[13] It is also referred to as a whole; an integral, value-loaded cultural process encompassing the natural environment, social relations, education, production, consumption and wellbeing.[14]

The *Study Guide on Development* of the Food and Agriculture Organization (FAO) describes the nature of development as under:

> "The ultimate purpose of development is to provide everyone with ever-increasing opportunities for a better life. It, therefore, acquires an equitable distribution of income and other social resources in order to promote justice and efficient production, to raise levels of employment substantially, to expand and improve facilities for education, health, nutrition, housing and social and cultural well-being. The qualitative and structural changes that development thus imposes on society must go hand in hand with economic progress while racial, ethnic and social inequalities must be substantially reduced. These are decisive factors in hastening development...."[15]

The World Bank has similarly set six parameters for a community to call itself developed. These are: absence of **poverty**, low **mortality** rate for children and pregnant mothers,

---

Quasi-Vanishing Act", *Economic Development and Cultural Change,* 13 July 1965, pp.385-393.

13. Food and Agriculture Organization, United Nations, Rome, *Study Guide on Development*, Freedom from Hunger Campaign/Action for Development, p.5.
14. Dag Hammarskjold Report on Development and International Cooperation, "Introduction-To Set in Motion the Process of Change", *Development Dialogue,* 1975, p.7.
15. Food and Agriculture Organisation, United Nations, Rome, *Study Guide on Development*, Freedom from Hunger Campaign/Action for Development, p.5.

primary **education** for all, **health** for all, **gender** equality, **environment** protection with sustainable development.[16]

Perhaps, the simplest definition of development is given by Robert Chambers, for whom development means just **'good change'**. Development may entail disruption of established patterns of living. Nevertheless, over the long term it implies increased living standards, improved health, and well-being for all, and achievement of whatever is regarded as a general good for society at large.[17]

David Korten[18] has outlined a **people-centred vision of development** and the basis of it he describes as follows:

> "The survival of our civilization...depends on committing ourselves to an alternative development practice guided by the three basic principles of authentic development: justice, sustainability and inclusiveness. **Justice:** Priority must be given to assuring a decent human existence for all people; **Sustainability:** Earth's resources must be used in ways that assure the well-being of future generations; **Inclusiveness:** Every person must have the opportunity to be a recognized and respected contributor to family, community and society."

Dudley Seers[19] in his article *The Meaning of Development* suggested that "the realisation of the potential of human personality...is a universally acceptable aim", and development must therefore entail ensuring the conditions for achieving the aim.

---

16. Source: www.worldbank.org/data/dev/devgoals.html
17. Allen, Tim and Thomas, Alan (Eds.), "Meanings and Views of Development" by Alan Thomas, *Poverty and Development into the 21st Century*, The Open University in Association with Oxford University Press, 2000, p.23.
18. Korten, David, as quoted *Ibid.*, pp.32-33.
19. Seers, Dudley, "*The Meaning of Development*", Paper Presented at the Eleventh World Conference of the Society for International Development (New Delhi, 1969), pp.10-12.

The **first three conditions** are the capacity to obtain **physical necessities** (particularly food); a **job** (including studying, working on a family farm or keeping house); and **equality**, which should be considered an objective in its own right. Seers also recognised the political dimension and suggested **three more conditions** for development: participation in government; belonging to a nation that is truly independent, both economically and politically; adequate educational levels (especially literacy). Seers' formulation was designed to challenge the economic basis of the type of vision of development with the emphasis on productivity, growth, and increasing GNP per capita.

Alan Thomas[20] has advocated **human-needs centred development** by extending Seers' six conditions for development to a **list of nine**. These are: low levels of material poverty; low level of unemployment; relative equality; democratisation of political life; 'true' national independence; good literacy and educational levels; relatively equal status for women and participation by women; sustainable ability to meet future needs; and human security.

Similarly, Porter[21] defines development as a complex of three important criteria: **economically**, sharp and sustained increase in national product; **socially**, redistribution of national income on an egalitarian basis and incorporation of marginal masses into the money-economy; **culturally**, emergence of a new social image.

---

20. Allen, Tim and Thomas, Alan (Eds.), "Meanings and Views of Development" by Alan Thomas, *Poverty and Development into the 21st Century*, *op. cit.*, p.34.
21. Porter, as quoted in Bhose, Joel S.G.R., *NGOs and Rural Development: Theory and Practice*, Concept Publishing Company, New Delhi, 2003, p.57.

Reidar Dale's idea of development stands for improvements in the quality of life of people, extending much beyond direct gains from increased production of commodities and services. He supplements the idea of income distribution among people and employment to the concept of GNP per capita to make it more convincing as an **economic indicator** of development. Some more specific economic variables as stated by him are as follows: electricity consumption; newspaper reading; automobile ownership. He also indicates the common **social indicators** of development, which are as follows: average expected life length at birth; infant mortality rate; calorie consumption per capita; proportion of undernourished children; hospital beds, usually per 1,000 inhabitants; literacy rate; rate of enrolment in primary schools; proportion of houses with piped water; average number of persons per room. To the above parameters he adds the following **people- or society-related dimensions** of development:

- **Orientation of Mind**: perception of one's own position and opportunities in the society, being closely related to whether or to what extent one has a development strategy (as opposed to a survival strategy) for oneself and one's dependants;
- **Dependent vs. Independent Position**: degree and terms of indebtedness, degree of competition for scarce resources, degree of inequality in gender relations, etc. influencing the degree of freedom in making choices about aspects of one's life;
- **Marginalised vs. Integrated Position**: degree and terms of participation in markets, degree and terms of participation in political and social life, type and strength of economic and social security networks;
- **Degree of Freedom from Physical and Mental Violence**: the extent to which one may lead one's life without deliberate

maltreatment or fear of such maltreatment, within one's family and in the wider society;

- **Degree of Mental Satisfaction**: the degree of mental peace and the ability to enrich one's life through non-material stimuli.
- **Institutional Features of Societies:** Moreover, at any level in any society, the aforesaid categories are intertwined with institutional features of societies, such as laws and other legal institutions; organisation of political life; scope, range and importance of public and private development organisations; orientation, effectiveness and efficiency of public administration; institutional mechanisms for sustainable use of natural resources; etc.[22]

---

22. Dale, Reidar, *Organisations and Development, Strategies, Structures and Processes*, Sage Publications, New Delhi, Thousand Oaks, London, 2000, pp.17-35.

8

Rural Development: Concept

Rural development seeks to involve a process of transformation from traditionally oriented rural culture towards an acceptance and reliance on science and technology.

– *D. Ensminger*

Shiv Mehta, who has made important contribution on the study of rural development, defines the term 'rural' as an area differentiated from urban in terms of its geo-physical location, spatial distribution of households based on kinship-family ties and close interaction between individuals and families. Of a rural area, he adds, the occupational structure centers around agriculture, the informal clientele system is formalised through established traditions and institutions, control and authority is based on ascription, and the belief system on faith and conviction on religious ethics and themes.[1]

Another authority on the subject, I.S. Hooda, refers to rural as a rural society or an area marked off by villages lying **outside** the jurisdiction of municipal corporations or committees and classified **not** as urban areas. A rural society has a socio-economic structure that is different from urban society. Social structure of a rural society consists of institutions like

1. Mehta, Shiv R., *Rural Development Policies and Programmes: A Sociological Perspective*, Sage Publications, New Delhi, 1984, p.13.

caste, class, religion, family, community, status, power, domination and a variety of other social contracts. The rural economic structure is closely linked to the social structure.[2]

Having defined the terms 'development' in the preceding chapter and 'rural' in the foregoing paragraphs, the term 'rural development' needs some deliberations.

In the words of Robert Chambers, "Rural development is a strategy to enable a specific group of people, poor rural women and men, to gain for themselves and their children more of what they want and need. It involves helping the poorest among those who seek a livelihood in the rural areas to demand and control more of the benefits of rural development. The group includes small scale farmers, tenants, and the landless."[3]

James Copp[4] has defined 'rural development' as a process aimed at improving the well-being and self-realisation of people living outside the urbanised areas through collective effort. He further says that the ultimate target of rural development is people, and not infrastructure. According to him, one of the objectives of rural development should be to "widen people's range of choices".

For Lassey,[5] the focus of rural development should be on the preservation of ecological integrity with a view to providing a continuing supply of life-supporting resources; efficient and appropriate land use; healthy living conditions; aesthetically pleasing environment; effective social, economic, and

2. Hooda, I.S. (Ed.), "Rural Development: Some Conceptual Issues" by I.S. Hooda, *Rural Development: Theory and Practice*, Spellbound Publications, Rohtak, 1997, p.2.
3. Chambers, Robert, *Rural Development: Putting the Last First*, Longman, London, 1983. p.147.
4. James H. Copp, "Rural Sociology and Rural Development", *Rural Sociology*, 37, 4, December 1972, pp.515-533.
5. For details see William R. Lassey, *Planning in Rural Environments*, New York, McGraw Hill, 1977.

governmental institutions; improved human welfare in terms of a minimal economic and social level of existence; physical structures and adapted landscape of pleasing design; comprehensiveness, that is, an entire range of physical, biological and human factors in rural regions.

Compared to Copp and Lassey's definitions of rural development, Ensminger's description is quite simple. "Rural development," Ensminger opines, "seeks to involve a process of transformation from traditionally oriented rural culture towards an acceptance and reliance on science and technology."[6] On the contrary, Michael P. Tadaro's[7] definition is elaborate to the extent of providing clear dimensions of rural development. For him rural development encompasses: improvement in level of living, including employment, education, health and nutrition, housing and a variety of social services; decreasing inequality in the distribution of rural incomes and in rural-urban balances in income and economic opportunities; and the capacity of the rural sector to sustain and accelerate the pace of these improvement. He, accordingly, draws four key facets of rural development, which are described as follows: livelihood and income generation; infrastructure development; human/social development; empowerment.

Over the years, rural development has emerged as "a **strategy** designed to improve the economic and social life of a specific group of people – the rural poor. It involves extending the benefits of development to the rural population who seek a

6. Ensminger, D., "Rural Development: What Is It, Its Contribution in Nation Building", Paper presented in East-West Centre's Conference on Integrated Communication for Rural Development, Honolulu, 1974, as quoted in Mathur, B.L., *Rural Development and Cooperation*, RBSA Publishers, Jaipur, 1996, p.5.
7. For details see Todaro, Michael P., *Economic Development in the Third World*, 3rd Edition, Longman Inc., New York, 1985.

livelihood in the rural areas."[8] John C. Ickis has identified three basic strategies, namely, growth, welfare, and responsive strategies:[9]

- **Growth-oriented strategy**: The role of the state in this strategy is to build infrastructure, and maintain a favourable climate to stimulate the growth of rural enterprises. The critical assumption of this strategy is that the benefits of increased production will gradually 'trickle down' to the poor.

---

8. *World Bank (1975): The Assault on World Poverty*, Johns Hopkins University Press, Baltimore, p.3.

   If rural development is so important, why is it not happening? Rural development has been neglected for many reasons: poor commitment and capacities in partner countries, waning international interest in rural issues, and poor commitment and weak past performance of the World Bank. Actions to address these causes of poor commitment represent the key components of this rural sector strategy. See *Rural Development – Vision to Action, A Sector Strategy*, The World Bank, Washington D.C., 1997, p.5.

9. Korten, David C. and Alfonso, Falipe B. (Eds.), "Structural Response to New Rural Development Strategies" by John C. Ickis, *Bureaucracy and the Poor: Closing the Gap*, West Hartford, Connecticut, Kumarian Press, 1993, Chapter 1.

   As a **concept**, rural development connotes overall development of rural areas with a view to improving the quality of life of rural people. In this sense, it is a comprehensive and multidimensional concept and includes the development of agriculture and allied activities – village and cottage industries and crafts, socio-economic infrastructure, community services and facilities, and above all, the human resources in rural areas. Rural development as a **method**, seeks people's involvement in all programmes. As a **process**, it seeks to modernize, through the application of science and technology, the traditionally-oriented rural cultures. Its major objective is to bring about improvement in the quality of life of rural people. See Satya Sundaram, I., *Rural Development*, Himalaya Publishing House, Mumbai/New Delhi/Nagpur/ Bangalore, 1997, p.5.

- **Welfare-oriented strategy**: This seeks to promote the well-being of the rural population in general, and the rural poor in particular, through large-scale social programmes. The primary means used in this strategy are free provision/distribution of goods, services and civic amenities in rural areas.
- **Responsive strategy**: This is aimed at helping the rural people help themselves through their own organisations and other support systems. The role of the government is to facilitate the self-help efforts of villagers by providing technologies and resources that are not locally available.

The World Bank defines rural development as a strategy to improve the socio-economic life of a specific group of people called rural poor. The group includes small farmers, tenants and the landless. The objectives of rural development, therefore, extend beyond any particular sector. They encompass improved productivity, increased employment and thus higher incomes for target groups as well as minimum acceptable levels of food, shelter, education and health.[10] The World Bank holds the following vision of rural development:[11]

- Rural growth is widely shared with private and competitive agriculture and agribusiness as the main engines of growth.

---

10. *Rural Development: Sector Policy Paper*, World Bank, Washington D.C., 1975, p.3.

    Uma Lele has a very similar view. According to her, rural development is an improvement in the living standard of the masses of low income population residing in rural areas and making the process self-sustaining. For details see Lele, Uma, *The Design of Rural Development: Lessons from America*, John Hopkins, Baltimore, 1975.

11. *Rural Development – Vision to Action, A Sector Strategy, op. cit.*, p.4.

    Like the World Bank's vision, the Economic and Social Commission for Asia and Pacific (ESCAP) has determined six important criteria of rural development. They are: drawing the entire rural labour force into the mainstream of economic activity; realizing the creative energies of the rural people, checking the drift of the rural population to cities,

- Family farms and non-farm enterprises provide ample remunerative employment opportunities to men and women.
- Rural people manage the soils, water, forests, grasslands, and fisheries in a sustainable manner.
- Rural people are linked to well-functioning markets for products, inputs, and finance.
- Rural people have access to medical care, clean water and sanitation, family planning services, educational opportunities, and sufficient nutritious foods.
- Essential legal frameworks, public investment, and productive and social services are provided and financed in a decentralised and participatory manner.

---

enhancing participation of women and youth in the rural development process, improving the quality of life through integration between development and environment, and the all-round development of the rural population by tapping the abundant manpower. See Sharma, S.K. and Malhotra, S.L., *Integrated Rural Development: Approach, Strategy and Perspectives*, Abhinav Publications, New Delhi, 1977, p.68.

9

Rural Development in India

The influence of Gandhi has led the participatory approach to development towards community development. The following equation explains the position well: basic needs+participatory development= community development (over a period of 25 years).

– ***Robin Poulton and Michael Harris***

Rural Development in Ancient India

The concept of village and its all-round development is found in the Vedic and later Vedic literature.[1] The Vedas declare need to strengthen life at three stages: *Brahma, Kshatra* and the People.

The *Rig Veda* in one of its verses says:

> Strengthen the power of knowledge/and strengthen minds/Strengthen the ruling power *(Kshatra)*/and strengthen heroes/Give strength to the milch-cows/and strengthen the people.[2]

1. Pandey, K.C., *Rural Development in Modern India*, B.R. Publishing Corporation, New Delhi, 1986, p.2.
2. *Rig Veda* VIII 35 16-18. Translations by A.C. Bose quoted in Pandey, K.C., *op. cit.*, p.1.

The *Yajur Veda* reads:

> Where *Brahman* and *Kshatra* both/move together in concord/ That world I shall know as one of bliss/where gods with *Agni* dwell.[3]

Manu, the Hindu law-giver, in his writings (200 B.C. – 2nd Century A.D.) said that a village was the fundamental unit of administration with its own officers and organisations.[4] It was the basic unit in ancient India that functioned for rural development.[5] From a religious point of view, ancient India was fundamentally individual-centric.[6] However, Rishis,[7] who were "worldly men, mixed and married with people, shared property and were of the people" initiated into acts of piety and social service, made all-round development of villages possible.

The Vedic prayer, *sarve sukhinah santu, sarve santu niramayaha,* i.e., may all be happy and healthy, highlight the universal dimension of development.[8] The Vedas speak of the cosmic order (order in nature), the moral order (relationship of man with others) and the social order (the actions of man in

---

3. *Yajurveda* 2V SXX 25 Translations by A.C. Bose quoted in Pandey, K.C., *op. cit.,* p.1.
4. Dube, S.C., *Indian Village,* Routledge and Kegan Paul Ltd., London, 1965, p.2.
5. Biswal, Purusottam, *Rural Development through Nationalised Banks in Orissa with Special Reference to Cuttack District (1969-1984),* Thesis submitted to Utkal University for Degree of Philosophy in Public Administration, Department of Political Science, Utkal University, Bhubaneswar, 1988, p.75 (Unpublished).
6. Jayaswal, K.P., *Hindu Polity,* 3rd edition, Bangalore Printing and Publishing Co., Bangalore, 1955, p.14.
7. Mazumdar, R.C. and Pusalkar, A.D. (Eds.), *The Vedic Age,* Allen and Unwin, London, 1957, p.354.
8. Singh, Katar, *Rural Development: Principles, Policies and Management,* Sage Publications, New Delhi/Beverly Hills/Newbury Park/London, 1986, p.20.

society). It contained prayers for "common place, common assembly, common thought".[9] 'common aim and common mind".[10] The *Upanishads* too emphasise the importance of development of the total human personality which develops when human beings live together and work for a common ideal. The *Sabha* of the Vedic period, reflecting these ideas, was both a village social club as well as a village council. *Jatakas* inform us that the villages transacted their business themselves. They enjoyed a high degree of decentralisation and autonomy. They used to organise work of charity and public utility.[11]

The four-fold objectives of life were: *Dharma, Artha, Kama* and *Moksha.*[12] The Vedas exhorted people to grow more food for their prosperity. They advocated sharing of food with the needy and glorified non-possession.[13] The emphasis was on development of self and community. Both wealth and ethics were shown as having importance to life.[14]

The common grounds of Buddhism, Jainism and teachings of Tirthankars of ancient India were that the whole world is a family and the prosperity of one is linked to that of the other. They contained the concept of rural development in an embryonic from. Many princes and merchants of idealistic frame of mind executed these ideas into action, but they left no

9. Siviah, M., Rao, K.V.N., Murthy, L.S.N. and Mallikarjuniah, G., *Panchayati Raj: An Analytical Study,* National Institute of Rural Development, Hyderabad, p.3.
10. Altekar, A.S., *State and Government in Ancient India,* 3rd edition, Motilal Bangaswami, Delhi, 1958, p.229.
11. Pandey, K.C., *op. cit.,* p.2.
12. Aiyanger, K.V. Rangaswami, *Aspects of Ancient Indian Economic Thought, Manindra Chandra Lectures 1927,* Banaras Hindu University, Banaras, 1934, p.22.
13. Pandey, K.C., *op. cit.*, p.3.
14. Manu, Chapter 3, Sloka 95, chap 4, Sloka 3, 8 and 12 as quoted in Pandey, K.C., *op. cit.,* pp.2-3.

organisational apparatus behind to carry on the welfare work beyond their lifetime. The life of the programme coincided with that of the benefactors.[15]

The excavations at Harappa and Mohenjodaro revealed how in the pre-historic period development was conceived through proper town planning, among other things, in the Indus Valley.[16]

Rural Development in Medieval and British India

The introduction of urban-oriented military-cum-landed elite called Mansabdar during the Mughal period gave a death blow to the concept of village autonomy. Introduction by the East India Company of landlord and Ryotwari systems as against the Mauzawari or village tenure system of earlier eras destroyed the communal life of the village folk. The position changed for the better under the British Crown.[17] The Manchester Cotton Supply Association took an interest in agricultural improvement in India, and advocated for establishment of a special Department of Agriculture in each of the provinces in British India.[18] During the 19th century, the Christian missionaries played an active role in rural regeneration. The missionaries initiated definite steps for economic and social uplift of their converts, through the most common way of settling them on land, employing them in factories and workshops which were started for the purpose. This led to a positive contribution towards improvement of Indian farming and village life.[19]

---

15. Pandey, K.C., *op. cit.*, p.3.
16. Ghosh, N.N., *Early History of India,* The Indian Press, Allahabad, 1964, p.16.
17. Malaviya, H.D., *Village Panchayats In India,* All India Congress Committee, New Delhi, 1970, p.145.
18. Bhattacharya, S.N., as quoted by Biswal, Purusottam., *op. cit.*, p.77.
19. Caray, William, as quoted by George Smith, *Life of William Caray,* Everyman's Library, London, pp.60-62 and 278.

In the princely states, rural reconstruction experiment was started by Maharaja Sayyaji Rao Gaekwad III over the whole State of Baroda in 1885. The basic approach to rural upliftment adopted by him was collaborative working of different departments with the people, which resulted in achieving success.[20] In course of the British rule, steps were taken in improving the economic standards of the rural farmers. The government adopted the system of advancing *Takkavi* loans to proprietors, farmers, subordinate tenants and ryots for embankments, tanks, water courses, etc.[21] Lord Curzon took a number of steps like application of scientific method to agriculture and establishment of a research institute and agricultural college for realising agricultural development in India.[22]

The non-cooperation resolution of Calcutta session of the Congress in September 1920 articulated the approach to rural development by recommending hand-spinning in every house and hand-weaving on the part of the millions of weavers who had abandoned their ancient and honourable calling for want of encouragement.[23] The spinning wheel economy adopted at this time by the Mahatma was the first popular exercise in rural development in India. Besides, the Mahatma designed a comprehensive programme of rural development which included the use of *khadi*, promotion of village industries, eradication of untouchability, provision of basic and adult education,

---

20. For details see Kavoori, J.C. et al., *History of Rural Development in Modern India*, Vol. I, Impex India, New Delhi, 1967, pp.28-88.
21. *The Report of the Royal Commission on Agriculture in India*, Government of India, 1928 p.417.
22. Maheswari, S.R., *Rural Development in India: A Public Policy Approach,* Sage Publications, New Delhi, 1985, p.24.
23. Sitaramayya, Pattabhi, *The History of Indian National Congress (1985-1935),* Working Committee of the Congress, Allahabad, 1935, p.342.

prohibition, women's uplift and the propagation of the national language.[24]

While Gandhiji tried to achieve rural development through a system of self-supporting and self-governing villages,[25] Rabindranath Tagore worked for integrated rural development through promoting consciousness among the rural people regarding their problems.[26] Tagore set up the Sriniketan Institute for Rural Reconstruction in 1921 with the aim of making rural population self-reliant and self-respectful.[27] In the same year Martandam experiment was started in Kerala under the leadership of Spencer Hatch of the Young Men's Christian Association 'to bring about a complete upward development towards a more abundant life for rural people, spiritually, mentally, physically, socially and economically'.[28]

These were entirely voluntary efforts but succeeded in drawing the government's attention to villages. A most notable name in this respect is F.L. Brayne, who started in 1927 a programme of rural reconstruction based on the old-fashioned virtues of hard work, thrift, self-respect, self-control, self-help, mutual help, and mutual respect.[29] The Firka Development Scheme was operational under the guidance of T. Prakasam.

---

24. Maheswari, S.R., *op. cit.,* p.25.
25. For details see Gandhi, M.K., *Constructive Programme – Its Meaning and Place,* Navajivan Publishing House, Ahmedabad, 1984, pp.8-30.
26. Dasgupta, S., *A Poet and a Plan in History of Rural Development in Modern India*, Vol. IV, Institute of Gandhian Studies, Varanasi, 1976, pp. 219-220.
27. Sriniketan Bulletin, No.11, 1946 as quoted in Maheswari, S.R., *op. cit.,* p.25.
28. Randhawa, M.S., *Developing Village India*, Orient Longman, Bombay, 1951, pp.39-42.
29. F.L. Brayne was the District Collector, Gurgaon who experimented with rural development in Gurgaon in 1920. See for details Brayne, F.L., *Better Villages*, Oxford University Press, Bombay, 1946, p.268.

Some more pioneering works included the Indian Village Service of the Wisers in Etah of Uttar Pradesh, the pilot project of Albert Mayer in Etah, the Nilakari experiment of S.K. Dey, and the Baroda, Bombay and Bihar State Rural Development Programmes. Similarly, in 1932 the princely State of Baroda launched a broad-based programme of rural amelioration to promote the will to live better and a capacity for self-help and self-reliance.[30]

Rural Development in Independent India

Development of rural areas is important for India because nearly 78 per cent of the population lives in villages and the development of India, by and large, lies in the development of its rural population. India's rural population is concentrated in village settlements, numbering nearly six lakhs.[31]

In the context of modern India, 'rural development' is defined as integrated development of area and the people through optimum development and utilisation (and conservation where necessary) of local resources – physical, biological and human, and by bringing about necessary institutional, structural, and attitudinal changes by delivery of a package of services to encompass not only the economic field, i.e., agricultural, allied activities, rural industries, but also establishment of required social infrastructure and services in the areas of health, nutrition, sanitation, housing, drinking water and literacy, with ultimate objective of improving quality of life of the rural poor.[32]

---

30. Maheswari, S.R., *op. cit.*, p.25.
    Also see Bhose, Joel S.G.R., *op. cit.*, p.70.
31. Mehta, Shiv R., *Rural Devclopment Policies and Programmes – A Sociological Perspective*, *op. cit.*, p.23.
32. Patel, A. R., "Rural Development – A Challenging Task For Voluntary Agencies", *Kurukshetra*, Vol.34(1), New Delhi, October, 1985, p.24.

Satya Sundara covers the following aspects under 'rural development' in the Indian context:[33]

- Changing the attitude of rural people towards development or transformation of village community;
- Promotion of democratic leadership at the grassroots level by setting up local self-governments;
- Provision of basic needs such as drinking water, healthcare, better sanitation, housing and employment;

---

33. Satya Sundaram, I., *op. cit.*, p.6.

Katar Singh explains the goals of rural development stating that they are designed to improve the conditions under which rural people work and live. The goals of policies are governed by what people desire, and the measures of policies, by what people think the government can and ought to do to bring about the desired change. This is the theory of public policy. Changes are desired only when people do not like the way things are going. Pressure for public action arises when people feel that they, individually, cannot bring about the desired adjustments. They have in mind some 'norm,' some image of an ideal situation towards which they strive. These norms become the goals of policy towards which objectives of specific programmes are directed. See Singh, Katar, *op. cit.*, pp.110-115.

Rural development is basically concerned with improving the standards of the mass of the low income population residing in rural areas and making the process of their development self-sustaining. Rural development involves changes in attitudes, customs, beliefs and values, output – both quantitatively and qualitatively, utilisation of natural and human resources, employment patterns and magnitudes, technology, institutional and organisational frameworks, incomes, both spatial and social relationships, rural lifestyles, and policy initiatives related to land and water, forests, inputs, supporting services, prices, backward areas and deprived sections of society, organization and administration, resource generation, self-sufficiency and self-sustenance, gender issues, sustainability, and management/conservation, government interventions, people's involvement, and the nature. See Mathur, B.L., *Rural Development and Cooperation*, RBSA Publishers, Jaipur, 1996, p.7.

- Development of both farming and non-farming activities so as to generate gainful employment without adversely affecting the environment;
- Improving infrastructural facilities in villages, particularly transport and communication facilities; and
- Ensuring a smooth life for the rural population by promoting communal harmony and unity, literacy, education and cultural activities.

The National Bank for Agriculture and Rural Development Act, 1981 of the Government of India defines **rural development** as development of rural areas through any activities conducive to such development, and activities conducive to development of rural areas include activities relating to production of goods or provision of services in rural areas and activities for the promotion of cottage and village industries, industry in the tiny and decentralised sector, and small scale industry and handicrafts and other crafts. **Rural areas** are defined, in the said Act, as the areas comprised in any village, and includes the area comprised in any town, the population of which does not exceed fifty thousand or such other figure as the Reserve Bank may specify from time to time.[34]

No programme was undertaken by any pre-Independence government so much in detail touching all rural areas of the country as it was done after the British handed over the reins of power to Indians.[35] After Independence, India initiated steps in a planned manner to promote rural development. While in the voluntary sector rural reconstruction in the lines of the works of Mahatma Gandhi was carried forward by many an agency generating a village centred movement, the Government of

34. *The National Bank for Agriculture and Rural Development Act, 1981, (61 of 1981)* Chapter I, Preliminary, Section 2.
35. Pandey, K.C., *op. cit.*, pp.64-65.

India launched the First Five-Year Plan in 1951, and in 1952 the National Community Development Programme (NCDP) to develop villages in a serious and coordinated way.[36] The National Extension Service was launched in 1953 to provide the essential staff to associate in rural development. In 1960 the government started Intensive Agricultural District Programme to attain, among others, food grain self-sufficiency. Thereafter, Growth Centre Strategy was set off which worked on the principles of clusters in order to further intensifying development. Planners realised the need for integration of all activities undertaken in an area, and the offshoot was Integrated Rural Development Programme. Latest addition is micro-level planning for rural development. This envisages local level planning based on locally available resources and needs.[37] Some of the government sponsored rural development programmes, *inter alia*, in accordance with their importance are discussed in the following section.

---

36. For details see Satya Sundaram, I., *op. cit.*, pp.10-17.

    Community Development was tested first on a pilot basis in Etawah by Albert Mayer, an American engineer and architect. See Mehta, Shiv R., *Rural Development Policies and Programmes – A Sociological Perspective*, *op. cit.*, p.24.

    Pandit Nehru called it a revolutionary programme due to the sheer size of the programme unsurpassed in any other country. See for details Mukherjee, B., *Community Development in India,* Orient Longmans, 1961, p.18.

37. *Ibid.*

    Also see Mitra, S.K., "Rural Development: Need for Holistic Approach," *The Economic Times,* November 21, 1992.

    For more details on micro-level planning see Planning Commission, *Report of the Working Group on Block Level Planning*, pp.3-4 and 16; and Misra, R.P. and Sundaram, K.V., *Multi-level Planning and Integrated Rural Development in India,* Heritage Publishers, New Delhi, 1980, p.20.

Rural development policies[38] followed in India can be classified into seven categories on the basis of the problem area to which a particular policy addresses itself. They are as under: land policy, forest policy, input policy, supporting services policy, price policy, policy of development of backward areas and the underprivileged and weaker sections, and policy for organisation and administration of rural development.

In every Five-Year Plan the Government of India adopted either a fresh policy of rural development or substantially fine-tuned the rural development programmes. While the **First Plan** (1951-56) put emphasis on community development as method and National Extension Services as an agency,[39] the **Second Plan** (1956-61) introduced cooperative farming and later local participation. The **Third Plan** (1961-66) was famed for introduction of the *Panchayati Raj* – three tier model of democratic decentralisation. **Three Annual Plans** followed thereafter which popularised and implemented new technology in agriculture. The **Fourth Plan** (1969-74) introduced special clientele-based and area-based programmes. The **Fifth Plan** (1974-79) had the concept of basic minimum needs borrowed from International Labour Organisation. The **Sixth Plan** (1980-85) included measures for strengthening the socio-economic infrastructure in rural areas, alleviating rural poverty and reducing regional disparity. Integrated Rural Development Programme was introduced during this plan period. The **Seventh Plan** (1985-90) gave emphasis to quickening the economic growth of rural areas, elimination of poverty and generation of productive employment. During the **Eighth Plan** (1992-97) emphasis was given on increasing productivity of

---

38. Singh, Katar, *op. cit.*, p.117.
39. Singh, Abha Lakshmi and Fazal, Shahab, *Agriculture and Rural Development*, B.R. Publishing Corporation, Delhi, 1998, p.25.

agriculture and enlarging the income of farmers by encouraging diversification into allied activities. The **Ninth Plan** (1997-2001) put emphasis on rural development through Self-Help Groups and *Swarnajayanti Gram Swarojgar Yojna* was introduced.[40] The **Tenth Plan** (2001-2006) strengthened implementation of SGSY as a comprehensive programme to remove rural poverty and emphasised on building rural connectivity for all-round development of villages.[41]

Notable Rural Development Initiatives

The themes of the major rural development programmes undertaken by the Government of India during the Five-Year Plans have been dealt hereunder.[42]

First Five-Year Plan (1951-56)

Bhoodaan and Gramdaan Movements

The *Bhoodaan* movement was started on 1951 under the leadership of Vinoba Bhave. Its aim was to acquire surplus land through donation from individual landowners and to distribute the acquired land among the landless families. Next year, the *Gramdaan* programme was started which had similar objectives. Such programmes had very little impact on the development of rural areas chiefly because the programmes lacked a broad based strategy and depended on voluntary nature of man for its success.[43]

---

40. Source: Bhose, Joel S.G.R., *op. cit.*, pp.77-78 and Singh, Abha Lakshmi and Fazal, Shahab, *op. cit.*, pp.24-59.
41. www.pmgsy.nic.in/
42. A list of important rural development programmes implemented in India after Independence, from First to Tenth Five-Year Plan, is given in **Annexure II**.
43. Singh, Abha Lakshmi and Fazal, Shahab, *op. cit.*, p.25.

National Community Development Programme

The National Community Development Programme (NCDP) was launched in 1952 – its aim being to bring about the overall development of the rural community with the people's participation in the development process. The government, on its part, provided technical and other services in a coordinated fashion. An institutional structure was provided in the form of *Panchayati Raj*, co-operative and village schools. The approach to the rural development was holistic. The objectives of the programme were, among others, raising food and other agriculture production, improving effectiveness of farm inputs, supply systems, providing agri-services to farmers and to develop local leadership and self-governing institutions. NCDP failed due to lack of funds, adequate implementing staff and absence of popular participation; yet the structure of country's future rural development administration was laid by establishment of Blocks as units of development.[44]

National Extension Service

National Extension Service (NES) was launched in 1953 to provide the essential staff to Community Development Blocks for extending community services including agricultural extension to the village folk for overall development of the area. The work involved not only education of the rural people in determining the problem, but also to suggest method for solution and, in the process, inspiring them towards positive action. Though the plan for NES was mooted in a grand way, its implementation necessitated huge amount of funds and trained and equipped staff which the government's revenue could not sustain.[45]

44. *Ibid.*, pp.25-26.
45. *Ibid.*, pp.8-12 and 26.

Second Five-Year Plan (1956-61)

Panchayati Raj

Pursuant to a study undertaken by a team headed by Shri Balwant Rai Mehta to examine Community Development Programme at the behest of Planning Commission[46] and its recommendation for local democracy, Rajasthan and Andhra Pradesh were the first states to introduce *Panchayati Raj* in 1959. Institutions under the *Panchayati Raj* were conceived as a process of democratic decentralisation for bringing about socio-economic development of rural areas. The system has been expanded form time to time.[47]

Package Programme

A package programme was worked out in 1960 for improving the agricultural practices in selected districts through the use of improved seeds, fertilizers, agricultural implements, etc. and the package of agro-services with the provision for competent technical advice, provision for credit and production supplies, storage, and to a limited extent development of roads.[48]

Intensive Agricultural District Programme

The Intensive Agricultural District Programme (IADP) was launched in 1960 aimed at concentrating resources in agriculturally better placed areas. It is a package programme with a district as focus. "It represented a significant departure from the approach adopted under NCDP: IADP employed concentration principle in deployment of resources as opposed to the equity

---

46. On 12 January 1958, the National Development Council approved of the recommendations of the Mehta Committee.
47. *Ibid.*, p.27.
48. *Ibid.*, pp.27-28.

criterion used in the NCDP."[49] The objective was to attain food-grain self-sufficiency in the shortest time. The programme was successful, but the success was location specific.[50]

Third Five-Year Plan (1961-66)

Rural Industrial Projects Programme

The Rural Industrial Projects Programme was initiated as centrally sponsored scheme by Planning Commission in 1962 to evolve appropriate methods and techniques for intensive development of village and small industries. The thrust of the programme was on effective promotion of cottage and small industry in rural areas to solve the problems of unemployment, under-employment and poverty.[51]

Hill Area Development Programme

The strategies of development adopted so far in the past led to an uneven distribution of the benefits of development between geographical areas and also between socio-economic groups. In response to that realisation certain area-specific programmes, such as Hill Area Development Programme (HADP), were initiated in 1962 during the Third Plan. The major emphasis of the programme was reduction of intra-regional and inter-regional differences in the distribution of benefits from agricultural development.[52]

Tribal Area Development Programme

The Tribal Area Development Programme (TADP) was commenced in 1962. It aimed at an integrated development

---

49. *Ibid.*, p.28.
50. Satya Sundaram, I., *op. cit.*, pp.12-13.
51. Singh, Abha Lakshmi and Fazal, Shahab, *op. cit.*, p.29.
52. *Ibid.*, pp.29-30.

programme for the administrative unit areas with 50 per cent or more of tribal concentration. The programme was specially designed to suit the communities living in those areas and to incorporate the special problem issues, like the problem of shifting cultivation.[53]

Applied Nutrition Programme

The programme was introduced in 1963 through an agreement with International bodies like FAO, WHO, UNICEF. The same was taken up with the objectives to wipe out the existing malnutrition from the rural areas caused due to calorie-protein, iron and Vitamin A deficiencies, and to enhance the socio-economic status of the rural population and to augment food production.[54]

Intensive Agricultural Area Programme

IADP was expanded to areas having high agricultural production potential with the Intensive Agricultural Area Programme (IAAP). The programme was launched in 1964 to ensure intensive development of important crops like wheat, paddy, millets, pulses, cotton, etc. in 114 select districts. Package approach to crop production was also adopted under the Area Programme which set the pace for introduction of HYV seeds leading to Green Revolution.[55]

High Yielding Variety Programme

In 1965, a distinctive strategy was adopted to increase agricultural production with the massive use of modern inputs, i.e., irrigation, chemical fertilizer, pesticides, new seeds, agricultural machinery, agri-credit from banks, etc. The government

53. *Ibid.*, pp.30-31.
54. *Ibid.*, p.31.
55. *Ibid.*, pp.31-32.

announced minimum support price and Food Corporation of India conceived and implemented purchasing of food grains from the market.[56]

Intensive Area Development Scheme

The Intensive Area Development Scheme (IADS) started in 1965 by a team sponsored by the Ford Foundation. It recommended the selection of certain areas for more intensive development. Districts with irrigation facility and assured rainfall were selected for IADS to boost their agricultural production. A district from every state was selected under the scheme.[57]

Three Annual Plans

The adverse economic situation in the country caused largely by severe droughts of 1966 and 1967 forced the government to declare a 'plan holiday' and in place of the regular five year plan, the country had three annual plans, i.e., 1966-67, 1967-68, 1968-69. Also, the sixties witnessed the Green Revolution consequent upon the introduction of new chemical fertilizers and high yielding seed varieties.[58]

Fourth Five-Year Plan (1969-74)

Growth Centre Strategy

If investment activities are intensified in a select area of a region, they will produce sufficient spread effect leading to the all round development of the region. Growth Centre Strategy was based upon the above principle, and the Fourth Plan a pilot project for growth centres was launched establishing 20 centres in different states. An attempt was made to intensify location-specific

56. *Ibid.*, p.32.
57. *Ibid.*, pp.32-33.
58. *Ibid.*, p.33

activities. The policy of growth centres is concerned more with development of areas rather than with their rates of growth. It is inapplicable in all development situations.[59]

Drought Prone Area Programme

A Rural Works Programme was started in 1967 in areas chronically affected by droughts with the principal objective of organising permanent works to obviate scarcity relief, and also to generate adequate employment through labour intensive schemes such as minor irrigation works, soil conservation, afforestation, etc. This programme was redesigned as Drought Prone Area Programme (DPAP) in 1970 with the objective of developing land, water, livestock and human resources of the identified drought prone areas.[60]

Crash Scheme for Rural Employment

The Crash Scheme for Rural Employment was taken up for implementation in 1971. The objectives were direct generation of employment in all districts of the country through execution of projects which are essentially labour intensive and production of assets of durable nature in keeping with local development. The weaker sections of the village community by and large benefited more than others under the scheme.[61]

Small Farmers Development Agency

The Small Farmers Development Agency (SFDA) scheme was introduced in 1971 with the objective of ameliorating economic condition of small farmers owning a landholding ranging from

---

59. Satya Sundaram, I., *op. cit.*, pp.13-14.
60. Singh, Abha Lakshmi and Fazal, Shahab, *op. cit.*, p.35.
61. Satya Sundaram, I., *op. cit.*, pp.240-242.

2.5 to 5 acres. Programmes based on land and animal husbandry were included in the project. Marginal Farmers and Agricultural Labourers Development Agency promoted interests of marginal farmers and agricultural labourers which acted on parallel lines that of SFDA.[62]

Tribal Area Development Programme

The Tribal Area Development Programme was started in 1972 under pilot basis in specified tribal areas with the objectives to minimise the gaps between the level of development among the tribal and non-tribal areas, and also to improve the quality of life of the tribal communities.[63]

Pilot Intensive Rural Employment Project

It was started in 1972 as an experiment in full employment. It aimed to provide full employment on such work projects not requiring skills of a high order in selected compact areas for creating durable assets that would have continuing multiple effect of creating new jobs; to impart new skill for selected workers to find out continuous employment in the secondary and tertiary sectors either in rural and urban areas.[64]

Fifth Five-Year Plan (1974-79)

Command Area Development Programme

The Command Area Development Programme (CADP) was introduced in December 1974. The focus of the programme was on the development of irrigation through levelling and shaping, land construction of field channels, introducing the *warabandi*

---

62. *Ibid.*, pp.247-250.
63. Singh, Abha Lakshmi and Fazal, Shahab, *op. cit.*, pp.36-37.
64. *Ibid.*, p.37 and Satya Sundaram, I., *op. cit.*, pp.242-244.

system of water management, and popularisation of integrated soil-crop water management practices.[65]

Minimum Needs Programme

The Programme was started in 1974 to improve the quality of life and also providing infrastructural facilities needed for supporting and supplementing the other beneficiary programmes like IRDP and TRYSEM, helping the rural poor. The main components of the programme include: elementary education, rural health, rural water supply, rural roads, rural electrification and nutrition.[66]

Twenty Point Programme

The Twenty Point Programme was initiated in 1975 with the basic objectives which include: to provide gainful employment in rural areas, help rural people acquire skill for gainful employment, to expose them to new technology to boost production, to arrest migration from rural to urban areas, to help rural families to come out of poverty within a short period.[67]

Food for Work Programme

This programme was introduced in 1977 as an integral part of the strategy to tackle the problem of rural employment and poverty to raise purchasing power with the rural people. The advantage of the programme was part payment of wage in food grains at subsidised prices to the target people which assured minimum nutrition to them. The work taken up under the scheme was aimed at creating durable community assets and strengthening the rural infrastructure.[68]

---

65. Singh, Abha Lakshmi and Fazal, Shahab, *op. cit.*, p.39.
66. *Ibid.*, pp.39-40.
67. *Ibid.*, pp.40-41.
68. Satya Sundaram, I., *op. cit.*, pp.251-353.

Integrated Rural Development Programme

The programme, abbreviated as IRDP, was launched in 1979 to improve the economic and social condition of the poorest section of rural society. It aimed at raising their levels of living and bringing them above the poverty line on a lasting basis by giving them income generating assets, credit facilities and other inputs. This happened to be the largest rural development programme the Government of India ever launched after Independence.[69]

Training of Rural Youth for Self-Employment

A national scheme for Training of Rural Youth for Self-Employment (TRYSEM) was launched in 1979, which aimed at equipping the rural youth with necessary skills and technical knowledge with a view to enabling them to seek self-employment. The scheme also envisaged backward and forward linkages to the trainees to work as successful entrepreneurs in rural areas.[70]

Antyodaya

Realising the limitations of the rural development programmes in conferring benefits on the poor, the Government of Rajasthan launched *Antyodaya* in 1977. It was subsequently expanded to 7 other states. *Antyodaya* means raising or lifting the last man.

---

69. Singh, Abha Lakshmi and Fazal, Shahab, *op. cit.*, pp.44-45.

    For details see Seetharam, M., "Integrated Rural Development: Trends and Challenges", *Kurukshetra,* November 1989, p.33.

    Mathew, T. (Ed.), "Integrated Rural Development: Concept, Theoretical Base and Contradictions" by G. Parthasarathy, *Rural Development in India,* Agricol Publishing Academy, New Delhi, 1981, p.30.

70. Singh, Abha Lakshmi and Fazal, Shahab, *op. cit.*, p.45 and Satya Sundaram, I., *op. cit.*, pp.298-305.

Special features of the programme include involvement of village representatives in identifying *Antyodaya* families and laying emphasis on economic criterion for selection of families without consideration of caste, colour and religion.[71]

Sixth Five-Year Plan (1980-85)[72]

National Rural Employment Programme

In short called NREP, was launched in 1980 in place of Food for Work Programme. The programme objectives were: to generate additional gainful employment, to create durable community assets, and to improve nutritional standard of the poor. NREP could stabilise wages in rural areas and created a wide variety of community assets.[73]

Development of Women and Children in Rural Areas

This was launched as a sub-scheme of IRDP in 1983 in all states of the country. The thrust of the programme was to cover the women from the families below poverty line residing in rural areas by organising them into groups and enabling them to take up activities which would help them to increase their income.[74]

Rural Landless Employment Guarantee Programme

The programme was launched in 1983 with the objective of improving and expanding employment opportunities for the

---

71. *Ibid.*, pp.244-250.
72. The Congress Party returned to power overthrowing the Janata Party, abrogated the Sixth Five Year Plan of the defeated government, and introduced its own Sixth Five-Year Plan (1980-85).
73. Singh, Abha Lakshmi and Fazal, Shahab, *op. cit.*, pp.47-48 Satya Sundaram, I., *op. cit.*, pp.253-257.
74. Singh, Abha Lakshmi and Fazal, Shahab, *op. cit.*, 1998, p.48.
    Satya Sundaram, I., *op. cit.*, pp.314-321.

rural landless and for creating durable assets for strengthening the rural economy. It differed from NREP by catering to the landless exclusively and providing guaranteed employment of 100 days.[75]

Seventh Five-Year Plan (1985-90)

Integrated Rural Energy Planning Programme

The Integrated Rural Energy Planning Programme consisted of development of institutional mechanism in the states/UTs, training, project preparation and implementation, provision of financial incentives, etc. regarding energy planning exercises in rural areas.[76]

Indira Awaas Yojna

To meet the housing needs of the rural poor Indira Awaas Yojna was initiated in 1985. It aims at helping rural people below poverty line belonging to SC and ST communities, freed bonded labourers and non-SC/ST category of people in construction of dwelling units and upgradation of unserviceable *kutcha* houses by providing grants-in-aid.[77]

Biogas Development Programme

The Biogas Development Scheme provided for technical design and support, training programmes, service facilities, repair and maintenance, central subsidy, etc. for promotion of biogas use

---

Dhillon, D.S. and Hansra, B.S., "On Making DWCRA Effective", *Kurukshetra,* September 1991, pp.25-26.

75. Singh, Abha Lakshmi and Fazal, Shahab, *op. cit.*, pp.48-49.
    Satya Sundaram, I., *Op. Cit.*, pp.257-259.
76. Singh, Abha Lakshmi and Fazal, Shahab, *op. cit.*, pp.53-54.
77. www.indianembassy.org (Chapter 17).

in rural areas. The scheme was a feature of the previous plan carried over to the Second Five-Year Plan.[78]

Rural Sanitation Programme

The programme was launched in 1986 with the objective of improving the quality of life of the rural people and to provide privacy and dignity to women. The concept was further expanded in 1993 to include personal hygiene, home sanitation, safe water, garbage, excreta and waste-water disposal.[79]

Jawahar Rojgar Yojna

The programme, called JRY in short, was launched in 1989 by way of merger of NREP and RLEGP. It was the most important scheme for employment generation meant for those below the poverty line. Projects like minor irrigation, rural roads, house site/construction, school/community building, social forestry, etc. were promoted under the programme.[80]

Eighth Five-Year Plan (1992-97)[81]

Crop Production Oriented Programmes

The Crop Production Oriented Programmes included the Special Food Production Programme for rice, wheat, coarse cereals, oilseeds, pulses, cotton, etc. Adequate emphasis was laid

---

78. Singh, Abha Lakshmi and Fazal, Shahab, *op. cit.*, p.55.
79. www.indianembassy.org (Chapter 17).
80. Satya Sundaram, I., *Rural Development*, Himalaya Publishing House, 1997, pp.260-270.

    Iyer, Paramesaran., "Creating Rural Employment: JRY's New Thrust Area", *Economic Political Weekly*, August 6, 1994, p.2065.
81. Due to political fluidity in the country with formation of successive short-lived governments of Mr. V.P. Singh and Mr. Chandrasekhar, launching of the Eighth Five-Year Plan was delayed by two years.

on horticulture crops. Programmes on Animal Husbandry, Dairy Development and opening of Krishi Vigyan Kendras (KVKs) or Farm Science Centres in districts were also initiated.[82]

Rajiv Gandhi National Drinking Water Mission

The National Drinking Water Mission was renamed as Rajiv Gandhi National Drinking Water Mission in 1991 after certain modifications. The Central Government supplements the efforts of the State Governments by providing assistance under the Accelerated Rural Water Supply Programme.[83]

Technology Development Extension and Training

Technological support is extremely vital for success of land based programme, especially in the development of wastelands. Proper area specific strategy has to be developed keeping in view the agro-climatic conditions and capability of land. Realising this, a Central Sector Scheme of Technology Development, Extension and Training (TDET) was launched in 1993 to develop suitable technologies for the reclamation of wastelands for sustained production of food, fuel wood, fodder, etc.[84]

Investment Promotion Scheme

The Investment Promotion Scheme for development of non-forest wastelands was launched in 1994 in order to stimulate involvement of the corporate sectors and financial institutions. The principal objectives of the scheme included the following to facilitate/attract/channelise/mobilise resources from financial institutions, banks, corporate bodies and

82. Singh, Abha Lakshmi and Fazal, Shahab, *op. cit.*, pp.58-59.
83. www.indianembassy.org (Chapter 17).
84. http://dolr.nic.in/tdet.htm

individuals for development of wastelands in non-forest areas belonging to the Central and State Government, *Panchayat*, village communities and private farmers; to facilitate production and flow of additional bio-mass including farm forestry products used as raw material for different types of industries and horticulture/commercial plantations.[85]

National Social Assistance Programme

The programme came into existence in 1995 to provide social assistance to poor households. It includes three benefits as its components: old age pension, central assistance in case of death of the principal breadwinner of the family and assistance to pregnant women under certain conditions.[86]

Integrated Wastelands Development Programme

The programme has been in implementation since 1995. Development of wastelands mainly in non-forest areas aimed at checking land degradation, putting such wastelands to sustainable use and increasing bio-mass availability. The programme aims at revitalizing and reviving village level institutions and enlisting people's participation.[87] It helps in generation of employment in rural areas besides ensuring participation in wastelands development programmes.[88]

Rural Sanitation Programme

The programme was modified in 1993, and the objectives were recast. The revised aim of the programme was: to raise sanitation coverage by a definite plan, to switch over from

---

85. http://dolr.nic.in/ips.htm
86. www.indianembassy.org (Chapter 17); http://rural.nic.in/nsap.htm
87. http://dolr.nic.in/iwdp1.htm
88. www.indianembassy.org (Chapter 17)

allocation driven programme to a demand driven programme, to shift from high subsidy to low subsidy regime, and ensure greater beneficiary participation and private sector involvement including greater NGO role.[89]

Ninth Five-Year Plan (1997-02)

73rd Amendment Act of 1992 on Panchayati Raj

The 73rd Amendment Act, 1992[90] provides constitutional status to the three-tier Panchayati Raj Institutions (PRIs). The Act envisaged *Panchayat* elections in every 5 years, reservation of seats for SC, ST and women (not less than 33 per cent), appointing State Finance Commission to recommend financial powers of the *Panchayat* bodies, constitution of District Planning Committee to prepare the draft copy of the District Development Plan, the powers of the *Panchayat* to levy taxes, duties, fees and tolls, etc.[91]

Jawahar Gram Samridhi Yojna

The Jawahar Gram Samridhi Yojna is the restructured form of the Jawahar Rozgar Yojna. Launched in 1999, it aimed at improving the quality of life of the rural poor by providing them additional gainful employment. The objectives were to create demand driven village infrastructure including durable assets for increasing the opportunities for sustained employment and generation of supplementary employment for the unemployed poor in rural areas.[92]

---

89. *Ibid.*
90. Came into effect in 1993.
91. www.indianembassy.org (Chapter 17)
    http://rural.nic.in/panch.htm
92. www.indianembassy.org (Chapter 17)

Employment Assurance Scheme

Though introduced in 1993, the programme was revised in 1999, and implemented in all the blocks of the country. It is now the single wage employment programme working with the focus in areas suffering from exodus of labour. The objective of providing employment in manual work to all needy able-bodied people of rural areas during the lean agricultural season, and the creation of community, social and economic assets for sustained employment and development.[93]

Swarnajayanti Gram Swarojgar Yojna

Popularly known as SGSY, it was launched in 1999 by merging IRDP, TRYSEM, DWCRA, Supply of Improved Toolkits to Rural Artisans (SITRA), and Ganga Kalyan Yojna (GKY). SGSY is a holistic programme covering all aspects of self-employment such as organisation of the poor into self-help groups, training, facilitating credit, technology, infrastructure and marketing. The objective of the programme was to bring the assisted poor families above the poverty line in three years, by providing them income generating assets through a mix of bank credit and subsidy provided by the government. SGSY also aimed at establishing a large number of micro-enterprises in the rural areas.[94]

Tenth Five-Year Plan (2002-07)

Pradhan Mantri Gram Sadak Yojna

The *Pradhan Mantri Gram Sadak Yojana* (PMGSY) was launched in 2000. The primary objective of the PMGSY was to provide connectivity by way of an all-weather road, to the

---

93. *Ibid.*
94. Source: Bhose, Joel S.G.R., *op. cit.*, pp.73-75; http://rural.nic.in/sgsy.htm

unconnected habitations in the rural areas, in such a way that habitations with a population of 1,000 persons and above are covered by 2003, and all unconnected habitations with a population of 500 persons and above by the end of the Tenth Plan.[95]

Sampoorna Grameen Rozgar Yojna

The *Sampoorna Grameen Rozgar Yojana* (SGRY) was started in April 2002. The primary objective of the Scheme was to provide additional wage employment in all rural areas and thereby provide food security and improve nutritional levels. The secondary objective was creation of durable community, social and economic assets and infrastructural development in rural areas.[96]

National Rural Employment Guarantee Act, 2004

This is an Act of the Government of India intended to safeguard the right to work of an individual by providing guaranteed employment at the statutory minimum wage to at least one adult per household who volunteers to do casual manual labour in rural areas. The Act gives effect to the provision under Article 41 of the Constitution of India, in terms of which, it is the duty of the State to provide employment to all its citizens. The application of this right is essential to ensure realisation of other constitutional rights such as right to life, right to food and right to education. The programme of guaranteed employment contributes to other important objectives such as infrastructural development, social equity, environmental protection and empowerment of women. As a decentralised approach to the provision of guaranteed employment, it would help to promote people's participation in development planning and local

---

95. http://www.pmgsy.nic.in/pmg31.asp#1
96. http://rural.nic.in/SGRY%20Guidelines%20-%20Final.htm

governance. The application of the Act extends to all rural areas of India. In terms of the Act, every household in the rural areas shall have a right to at least 100 days of guaranteed employment every year for at least one adult member, for doing casual manual labour at the statutory minimum wage, and to receive the wages thereof within 7 days of the week during which work has been done.[97]

An exhaustive list of developmental schemes in which Departments/Ministries of the Government of India seek collaboration with or provides assistance to NGOs is given in the end of the book in **Annexure III.**[98]

---

97. This has been borrowed from a paper prepared in 2004 by individual members/experts for discussion in the NAC (Government of India). WWW.Rural%20Employment%20 (2).
98. Collected from *Report of the Steering Committee on Voluntary Sector for the Tenth Five-Year Plan (2002-2007)*, Planning Commission, Government of India, January 2002, pp.34-39.

    For details on Government-NGO partnership, refer to *A Compendium of Partnership Between Government and Voluntary Sector* (All India Conference on the Role of the Voluntary Sector in National Development, 20th April, 2002 New Delhi), Planning Commission, Government of India, New Delhi.

10

NGOs: Role in Rural Development

Good and effective leadership is the last word on the subject of good governance, no matter if it is of government or nongovernment.

– ***Author's reflection***

This chapter is designed to present a case study on the role played by NGOs in Puri district of Orissa. Before the findings of the study are explicated, the historical growth of NGOs in Orissa and Puri district will be provided to the reader, in the same way as the growth of NGOs in the world and India has been laid out in chapter II, to facilitate better appreciation of the outcome of the study. An attempt is also made to brief the reader on the profile of the district and the sample area before the findings are elaborated.[1]

Growth of NGOs in Orissa

From ancient times there have been reformist trends in the religious and social life of people of Orissa. There have appeared from time to time reformers and religious teachers, including non-conformists, who have asserted the inner essence

1. The method of study has been dealt in detail in Annexure IV in the end of the book.

of people's life, such as love and fellow feeling. In the post-Vedic period' Mahavir and Goutama Buddha launched their movements offering people, among others, lessons on good life. In the middle ages, reformer saints like Kabir, Nanak, Sri Chaitanya, Shankar Dev, Jananadev and Narasingh Mehta made similar efforts. Orissa was greatly influenced by these movements. Sarala Das in the 15th century and the *Panchasakha,*[2] who emerged early in the 16th century, belonged to the indigenous category of the similar endeavours or movements that swept across Orissa and moulded the people's life and culture perceptibly.[3] In those days, in Orissa, the voluntary action was by and large an individual exercise generally lacking in the framework of organisation, but later in the late 19th century voluntary action led to setting up of organisations that worked for socio-economic and religious welfare of the people.

During the British rule, charitable organisations for health and education were promoted by the elite and the rich. After Independence, many nonprofit organisations were promoted in different parts of Orissa on Gandhian line. These organisations worked mainly in the field of basic education, sanitation, *Harijan* welfare, khadi, etc. Utkalamani Gopabandhu Das was in the forefront of the voluntary movement during the pre-Independence period. A professional body of social workers now leads most NGOs in Orissa, articulating the aspirations of its disadvantaged masses.[4]

---

2. Translated as "Five Friends", viz., Jagannath Das, Balaram Das, Achyutananda Das, Jasobanta Das and Ananta Das.
3. Lahiri, Aloka, "The Social Content of Panchasakha Movement", *Orissa Review,* Government of Orissa Press, April 2002, pp.49 to 54.

   For details also see Mahapatra, Sitakanta, *Jagannath Das*, New Delhi, 1989, and Das, Chittaranjan, *Balaram Das*, New Delhi, 1982.
4. Mohanty, Bimalendu, *Orissa Yesterday, Today and Tomorrow*, Nur Publishers, Bhubaneswar, 2003, p.133.

Orissa, like the rest of India, was vibrant with traditional or Gandhian voluntary organisations in 1950s and 1960s. The first ones were active in Koraput, Ganjam and Sundargarh districts, and were primarily engaged in land gifts (*bhoodaan*) and voluntary labour (*shramdaan*), etc. Later they took up issues like bonded labour, rights of the tribal people over forest products and sharecroppers' problems.[5] Nonprofit organisations like Ford Foundation, Oxfam and CARE have been active in Orissa since 1960s, bringing in international aid and expertise to the State.[6] In 1950s and 1960s a number of NGOs came up in the State, but most of them were active mostly in tribal and interior pockets of Orissa in building homes for the destitute. Two of the leading names of those days were Parbati Giri and Tulasi Munda. Malati Choudhury established Baji Rout Chatravas in a tribal area. In the interior and tribal dominated districts of Ganjam, Sundargarh and Phulbani, NGOs made tremendous sacrifices to bring developmental inputs to the people. The NGO leaders led Spartan lives and were inspired by lofty ideals.[7]

In 1970s welfare-based NGOs came up to fill the space created by government development schemes/programmes. There were others doing only relief-oriented activities. Their role was more like delivery agents in areas of health (mobile dispensaries and the like) and education. The NGOs adopted the approach of community control of management to the new projects in the later part of this decade. This gave birth to village level committees which functioned as forums to discuss modes of uplift of the village people themselves. The NGOs also

---

5. Pradhan, Jagdish, Panda, Bijoy and Menon, Geeta, *Facets of the Irony: Emerging Development Trends and Directions in Orissa,* Development Resource and Training Centre, CYSD, 1997, pp.30-31.
6. Mohanty, Bimalendu, *op. cit.,* p.134.
7. *Ibid.*, p.134.

promoted activities like encouragement of small savings, revitalising traditional systems (grain banks and tribal Panchayats), grassroots movement for forest protection etc.[8] The NGO sector in Orissa owes much of its maturity and professionalism today to the experience of these early campaigners. One of them is A.V. Swamy,[9] who initiated the Oxfam programme in south Orissa in mid-1970s. Another programme for voluntary action was initiated by PIDIT. These two projects led to the development of a cadre of trained, professional development workers, who branched out to form their own voluntary organisations.

In the meantime, another set of voluntary workers came from the programmes of the Catholic Church. Ex-PIDIT volunteers formed NIPIDIT[10] in Phulbani and PIPAR in Dhenkanal. The Gandhi Peace Centre, New Delhi, also promoted NGOs in different parts of northern Orissa. They gave these NGOs philosophical and financial support. The NGOs which came up with the support of the Churches were Gram Vikas, PREM, THREAD and REACH. Some of the important personalities who led this movement were Joe, Anthia Mediath and Jacob Thundy. These organisations brought environmental awareness and innovative ecological

8. Pradhan, Jagdish, Panda, Bijoy and Menon, Geeta, *op. cit.*, pp.30-31.
9. An engineer by training and Gandhian by action.
10. Ram Das and Raghunath established NIPIDIT in Phulbani to promote tribal people's action and protection of environment. PIPAR in Dhenkanal also works with the same objective. FARR and CYSD led by Pramila Pradhan and Jagadananda respectively have rendered yeoman's service for development of Orissa. Aditya Patnaik, a neo-Gandhian, of Antyodaya Chetana Mandal has established an eye hospital in remote Mayurbhanj and undertaken various integrated activities in different parts of Orissa. See Mohanty, Bimalendu, *op. cit.*, p.135.

projects to the State, like bamboo board, biogas, and vertical brick kilns.[11] Achyuta Das of Kasipur Block in Koraput was another leader who sacrificed his life for people's welfare. Ashok Nanda coming from the tradition of independent local movements funded VIKAS which was involved in the rehabilitation of the disabled and the lepers. VIKAS promoted an alternative model for micro-banking and forayed into waste management.[12]

The concept of people's participation in development programmes began to be talked about in 1980s. During this period there was a shift of funding priorities of donors and development agencies away from Tamil Nadu and Andhra Pradesh. Orissa was a beneficiary of the process. The floodgates were opened for NGOs of all kinds leading to a virtual NGO boom.[13] According to Lalit Mishra's *Status Report*, the factors were expansion of funding agencies, shifting in their geographical priorities, widening of scope of work by NGOs, potential of the voluntary sector to provide employment to people, exit of volunteers from large organisations forming their own NGOs.[14] In mid-1980s the professional NGO activity was promoted by Dr. Radhakanta Naik through NISWAS and

---

11. Mohanty, Bimalendu, *op. cit.*, pp.134-135.

    Gram Vikas developed an attractive campus at village Madhur near Berhampur, and it is in the forefront of rural development in Orissa now. PREM now works with around 15,000 families in the state and created a large woman's credit organisation called Utkal Mahila Sangathan. These organisations work on capacity building among rural poor. *Ibid.*, p.135.
12. *Ibid.*, p.136.
13. Pradhan, Jagdish, Panda, Bijoy and Menon, Geeta, *op. cit.*, pp.30-31.
14. For details see Mishra, Lalit, *Status Report on Non-Governmental Organisations in Orissa*.

Father Bogaert of Xavier Institute of Management, Bhubaneswar.[15]

In 1990s the NGO boom became even bigger due mainly to the persistence of the above forces as also the growing disenchantment with the government-led development work.[16] In 1993 Madhusmita Misra set up *Jeevan Rekha Parishad* working in the field of reproductive child health, environment protection, support to the disabled, and vocational training to women. She established Orissa Human Rights Forum in 1999 to focus on issues relating to women's rights. In 2002, Paresh Naik, a prominent social activist, established Orissa International Centre for Development of Orissa with contributions of Non-Resident Indians. He earlier established *Tathastu* and *Sukruti* which did useful work in education, health and environment.[17]

Among all the leaders of the NGO sector of the state since Independence, the names of three come out as most outstanding. They constitute a trio, namely **A.V. Swamy** of Oxfam fame, **Achyuta Das** of Kasipur and **Jagadananda** of CYSD. **Within the NGO sector, they are even respected as architects of modern voluntarism in Orissa.**[18] However, purely movement-based NGOs or NGO leaders are hardly found in Orissa.[19]

Funds Flow and Other Issues

Total volume of outside funds coming to Orissa NGOs has been estimated differently. According to *Rashtriya Sahara*

15. The information was gathered through visits to these institutions and discussing with the authorities concerned. These institutions also offer professional Social Science post-graduation courses.
16. Pradhan, Jagdish, Panda, Bijoy and Menon, Geeta, *op. cit.*, p.32.
17. *Ibid.*, p.37.
18. It is author's own assessment on the basis of discussions held with various leaders of the NGO movement in Orissa.
19. Pradhan, Jagdish, Panda, Bijoy and Menon, Geeta, *op. cit.*, p.33.

(September 23, 1995) estimate, the amount could be $30 million. Another source puts the figure at Rs. 35.28 crore in 1992-93.[20]

The biggest difficulty in identifying NGOs arises because they are registered under either the Societies Registration Act, 1860, or the Indian Trust Act, 1882, under which are registered a variety of establishments or agencies not having any objective of voluntary or social work. Besides youth clubs, religious outfits and small welfare organisations, it is estimated that there are nearly 5,000 NGOs in the state which have established offices and have regular staff. But those receiving foreign funds under FCRA are approximately 2,000 in number. There are many NGOs which are dependent on government funds. These are mostly new NGOs. Some are issue-based advocacy groups who do not rely much on outside funds and work at micro level.[21] The number of NGOs in the state, according to a source in Government of Orissa, stands at 5,817.[22] As per PDC Network Directory, there are currently 3,074 **development** NGOs operating in Orissa.[23]

NGOs now are courted actively by both government and corporate sectors to deliver development programmes to the disadvantaged. Liberalisation and globalisation have necessitated a move by both the agencies to seek out channels that could deliver development. NGOs are the vast repositories of development experience and expertise that could help to deliver development with sensitivity and equity.[24]

---

20. *Ibid.*, p.9.
21. *Ibid.*, p.32-33.
22. *Orissa Reference Annual, 2003,* Government of Orissa, Information and Public Relation Department, December 2003, p.324.
23. *Directory of Voluntary Organisations – Orissa 2004*, PDC – Network, Bhubaneswar, 2004.
24. Mohanty, Bimalendu, *op. cit.*, p.137.

Growth of NGOs in Puri District

Puri, by virtue of its being the seat of Lord Jagannath, has developed to be one of the most important places for voluntary social service organisations. The place has attracted many religious and philanthropic persons to establish charitable and social service organisations not only for the benefit of the devotees and pilgrims, but also for the helpless and afflicted persons. Thus, several organisations for orphans, forsaken women and widows, wandering ascetics and other welfare organisations have come into existence in Puri. Besides, *Dharmashalas* and dispensaries have also been established for the benefit of pilgrims and devotees. The names of the following organisations are prominent in the district: Puri Anathashram, Basantkumari Bidhabashram, Mahila Kutir Silpa Sikshashram, Lok Karya Kshetra, Bharat Sevashram Sangha, Nari Seva Sangha, Ramakrishna Mission Ashram, Youth Hostel Association of India, Nilachal Nari Seva Samiti, Puri Swasthya Pratisthan, Jara Nivas, and Orissa Jatiya Byayam Krida Parishad.[25]

According to a Government of Orissa publication, the district has 576 NGOs as of December 2003.[26] However, a PDC Network publication, which has compiled a directory of development NGOs[27] of the State, puts the figure at 248 for the district as in 2004.[28]

Eighty per cent of the development NGOs registered and functioning in Puri district was formed during 1980 to 1999.

---

25. Senapati, N. and Kuanr, D.C., *Gazetteer of India, Orissa, Puri*, Gazetteers Unit, Department of Revenue, Government of Orissa, pp.644-688.
26. *Orissa Reference Annual – 2003*, Government of Orissa, Information and Public Relation Department, December 2003, p.324.
27. NGOs engaged in development activities.
28. *Directory of Voluntary Organisations – Orissa 2004*, PDC – Network, Bhubaneswar, 2004, pp.425-465.

This implied that during 1980s and 1990s, there was an explosive growth of NGOs in Puri district as in the rest of Orissa and India. Between 2000 to August 2004, twenty-two development NGOs were registered. It so appeared that the momentum of growth during the new millennium abated a little.

The organisations, set up during the pre-Independence era and the period immediately following Independence, were mostly oriented to service and relief work such as orphan care, old age home, accommodation for helpless women and widows, facilities for the youth and stay arrangement for pilgrims, devotees and travellers. Some also involved themselves in sports, culture, religious activities, and during natural disasters (flood, cyclone, etc.), engaged in relief work, but there were hardly any NGOs, or activities undertaken by them, during the period prior to 1970 that could be categorised in the area of rural development in the district.[29] Furthermore, the number of organisations serving in their respective areas of activities was very small, and particularly, working in the field of rural development would be insignificant, compared to the growth and spread noticed in 1970s, and especially, the boom during 1980s and 1990s.[30] Presently, Puri district has a reservoir of development NGOs catering to rural development as their core function in tune with national and state concern for underdevelopment.

---

29. The conclusion is an outcome of the above data analysis.

30. This is the result of the analysis conducted in the preceding paragraph.

    This is not to deny that certain international NGOs, viz. Oxfam, CARE, etc. having their offices at State level had occasionally rendered some good service to people in rural areas, particularly in the field of nutrition support to school children and pregnant/nursing mothers. Though it is doubtful whether such programmes can be considered strictly as rural development activity, the programmes were too little to deserve further elaboration. See Senapati, N. and Kuanr, D.C., *op. cit.*

Profile of Puri District and Sample Area

The district was named after its headquarters town, Puri. The Government of Orissa reorganised the district into three separate districts in 1993. The undivided district of Puri is very rich in historical antiquities. The Chilka Lake is situated here. The total population of the district in 2001 was 1,502,682. The rural population of the district formed 86.42 per cent of the total population. There were 2,87,463 households, and the average household size was 5.2. The district comprised 11 Blocks, 4 towns and 1614 villages. The literacy rate was 78 per cent. About 65 per cent of the total population of Puri depended on agriculture. The total net sown area of the district was 1,33,580 hectares during 2000-01. The district suffered severe flood in 2000 and 2001. The super-cyclone of 1999 devastated its agricultural economy. The district is long famous for its traditional crafts and cottage industries. The number of villages electrified constituted 97 per cent of the total number of villages. The work participation rate stood at 30 per cent.

Puri Sadar was chosen as the area of study. It is one of the 11 Community Development Blocks of Puri district comprising 260.82 square kilometres, 16,105 households, 142 inhabited and 14 uninhabited villages, and 26 *Gram Panchayats*. Situated in the eastern parts of Puri district, a part of its flank is washed by the Bay of Bengal and the remaining shares the border with Puri town. To its west lies Satyabadi block, to the north is Gop block and to the south lies Bramhagiri block.

The Census of India 2001 carved out 11 sub-districts out of the district of Puri, and nine of them were named after the blocks of the district. The census data were prepared taking sub-districts into consideration. Although the area of Puri Sadar sub-district did not exactly coincide with that of the block, a major part of the sub-district was covered in the area of Puri Sadar block. While presenting population and socio-economic data, the census data of Sadar sub-district would be given in lieu of similar data of the block, which, being situated in the same region, largely reflected the socio-economic profile of Sadar block.

The total population of Sadar sub-district was 89,638 in 2001, of which 45,238 were males and 44,400 females. The entire population was rural. The population in the age group 0-6 stood at 11,650 (6,054 males and 5,596 females). The number of people in Scheduled Caste and Scheduled Tribe categories stood at 15,201 and 237 respectively. The average household size was 6.

The Census of India 2001 brought out certain significant information on living conditions of the people of Sadar *tahasil*[31] (which is an area slightly larger than the sub-district) that applied to the people of the sub-district as well. This information throws enough light on the level of people's development/underdevelopment and the need for a strategy to improve their lot through appropriate rural development activities.

Of 19,602 houses mentioned in the census report, 14,775 had grass/thatch roofs, 8,513 had mud walls, 11,932 had mud floors. Of the total of 16,395 households, only 2,690 had drinking water source within their premises and 5,654 had the such facility far away from the premises, 14,648 had no latrines with their houses, 12,584 used kerosene for lighting, 9,081 either had no kitchen or cooked in the open, 12,446 did not avail of banking facility and 12,121 did not even possess a radio/transistor, 14,406 had no TV, 15,986 had no telephone, 7,062 did not even have a bicycle for communication. The above analysis shows that poverty stalked the Sadar region of

31. Census of India 2001 shows Sadar sub-district with 16,105 households, Sadar *tahasil* with 16,395 households. Hence, Sadar *tahasil* covers 205 more households than the sub-district. For the purpose of the study the data can have analytical value.

the district; it required substantial efforts in rural development to improve the living standard of the people there and their environment.

Role of NGOs in Rural Development

Having dwelt on the conceptual aspects of NGOs and rural development in chapters 1 to 9 and on the growth of NGOs in Orissa and Puri district as also the profiles of Puri district and sample area in the beginning of this chapter, the role of NGOs in rural development can appropriately be examined now in the context of the findings emanating from the field study. The field study was conducted through circulation of two sets of questionnaires to the NGO and citizen respondents of the sample NGOs and citizens, and supplementary interview where necessary. The Annexure IV at the end of this book deals with the features pertaining to sampling and techniques adopted for data collection, selection and particulars of the sample villages, data analysis, etc. The present section will deal with the findings relating to the role played by NGOs in rural development.

A section above, devoted to growth of NGOs in Puri district, showed that 1980s and 1990s were the decades of explosive growth of NGOs in the district, as was the position in the state as well as in India, and the outside world. The NGO boom even continued thereafter in the new millennium though apparently with a lesser momentum. The district, in the process, had benefited to the extent of having 248 development NGOs set up mostly during the last 34 years with the avowed objective of contributing to rural development. The number thus formed the backbone of the civil society working and awaiting the opportunity to devote to rural uplift in and out of the district. Against this backdrop, the growth and spread of NGOs in Puri district was found satisfactory from the point of view of their numerical strength with a view to taking the responsibility of rural development in the district.

Number of NGOs working for a cause is as much important as structure of the agencies, for the structure or the architecture determines the capacity of an NGO to carry on an appointed task to the desired level of success. It was, therefore, considered appropriate to study this aspect while examining the role of NGOs in rural development. It has been shown in Chapter 3 that NGO structure includes, among other things, registration, General Body, Governing Body, Advisory Body, staffing pattern, etc. An attempt is, therefore, made below to analyse these aspects of the structure of NGOs.

It came to our notice that the structure of NGOs as society under the Societies Registration Act of 1860 was overly popular with NGO practitioners. While discussing its reason with respondents, it was gathered that the relative Act used for registration was comparatively simple, less cumbersome and relatively hassle free. This attracted the attention of NGO leaders to get registration of their organisations done under the said law.

Further, 63 per cent of NGOs held meetings of Governing Body twice or less in a year, and more than 80 per cent of NGOs conducted three or more meetings of the General Body in a year. It implied that the formality necessary for scrutinising NGO functioning was observed which had potential to ensure internal democracy in NGOs through members' scan of the organisational functioning periodically.

The importance of Governing Body to NGO has been discussed in Chapter 3. The Governing Council is the leadership of the NGO and akin to the steering wheel of a vehicle. It is expected to meet as many times as possible in a year to effectively control the working process of NGO. Contrary to this, it was observed that in case of most of the NGOs the Chief Functionary determined the the constitution of the Governing Body. The General Body, to all appearance, was only a necessity, though holding its meeting was only an empty ritual.

The collegial leadership through the form of Governing Body had a *de jure* existence, and the Chief Functionary was the *de facto* head. In an ideal situation, members of the Governing Body should have been elected by the General Body in keeping with democratic norms of the modern times. This finding of the study suggests the trend that NGOs were individual-driven organisations, wherein the Chief Functionary, instead of being delegated the power to function by the leadership, i.e., the Governing Body, wielded substantial influence to mould the organisation and conduct work in his/her terms. It looked like the proverbial tail wagging the dog instead of the dog wagging the tail.

Despite the fact that 86 per cent of NGOs were registered as society, which was supposedly a popular form of organisation for promoting democracy within the organisation, the NGOs were run autocratically by Chief Functionaries, and thus the supposed benefit of registration of NGOs as society did not accrue to the NGOs. Whether the trend was beneficial or not can only be judged from the degree of success these NGOs achieved in promoting their objectives.

Only 52 per cent of NGOs affirmed that their organisation did have an Advisory Body and the remaining ones did not have any. The above statistics suggested something very vital about NGOs, i.e., a large chunk of the NGOs (48%) did not have Advisory Body, meaning thereby that the role of experts and expertise of consultants had no relevance for nearly the half of the NGOs. Considering that about 88 per cent of the NGO leaders were simple graduates/post-graduates, only 4 per cent of the NGO leaders held some professional qualifications, and the remaining 8 per cent were mere under-graduates, there was a need for ideas and expertise for working out of projects, implementation of programmes, raising resources, management of organisations, etc. for NGOs. Giving professional orientation to

NGO management was found to be essential, which could come about only by ushering in ideas from subject experts.

A vast number of NGOs with Advisory Body received useful services from consultants. Those not benefiting from the existence of Advisory Body, constituted around 11 per cent of the total number of NGO respondents. As such, 54 per cent of all NGOs either did not have Advisory Body, or despite having it, informed of not receiving any benefits from the Advisory Body. The fact of not benefiting from Advisory Body appeared due to the incapacity of advisors to guide NGOs. This drove home the point that advisors or consultants could contribute to improving the functioning of NGOs only if they were professionally equipped.

Fifteen per cent of NGOs did not have any regular staff. The interpretation of it was that the NGOs falling in this slim category were small in operation, and hence, members themselves had to undertake the requirements of day-to-day administration and field responsibilities. The remaining 85 per cent of NGOs were relatively bigger in size due to higher level of operation undertaken by them which necessitated hiring of staff for administration and field work. Here, a conclusion could be drawn on the issue concerning the size of NGOs, namely that 15 per cent of the NGOs were minor players in the field of development. Further, absence of a very large number of administrative and field staff with NGOs indicated non-existence of big NGOs in the sample NGOs taken for study. It, therefore, seemed probable that big players of the voluntary sector were conspicuous by their absence in the field of rural development in the region.

Payments to the staff in accordance with industry standards, staff display of high level of commitment to work, and low turnover of staff are crucial to any organisation for success of its mission. The voluntary sector is no exception.

Contrary to a strong feeling within and outside NGOs of low pay to their field staff, the study furnished information to conclude that field staff in all likelihood were not generally paid below the market determined rate, i.e., the rate commonly accepted by NGOs for payment as compensation to their field staff; NGOs were aware of high commitment level of their field staff; and NGOs did not to a significant extent experience high turnover of field staff (implying that staff continuance on job was long-term). These findings together sent a message: NGOs having a complement of staff could be trusted with assignment of projects for doing a reasonably good job.

NGOs were averse to talking to outsiders on issues relating to their annual budgets and level of business. However, such particulars could give insight into the size of NGO operation. In the absence of NGO cooperation in this respect, an effort was made to ascertain the sources of NGOs' funds and the nature of constraints NGOs faced in raising funds for projects. It was found that State Government/Government of India grants and financial support of international agencies made up the major sources of funds of NGOs. In light of the above, it could well be argued that the future of NGO sector will be determined by these agencies through their purse strings. This had serious implications on the autonomy of the voluntary sector which will be discussed later in this chapter.

Organisations are created to discharge functions in achievement of their mission. NGOs being organisations also have to perform functions in conformity with objective which is their *raison d'être*. Functions lead to result, and result impacts society. It is the objective of the study to examine the result, i.e., in the instant case, rural development. It is, therefore, very vital to study functions of NGOs in all their ramifications.

In this connection, NGOs were asked how they viewed their role *vis-à-vis* the government which happened to be an all-pervasive player in the field of development in the Southern countries. Eighty-one per cent of NGOs reported to work with the government for provision of services, and it was found that NGOs were inclined to collaborate or work with the government in a similar fashion. A very small number of NGOs felt that they and the government were adversaries in light of the above, even though the state and its agencies in their part tried to associate NGOs in a number of rural development programmes. It was relevant to know whether NGOs had taken initiatives to ensure benefits of government sponsored development programmes to reach the people in an effective manner, and the nature of initiatives taken by them in this connection. A vast number of NGOs reported that they had taken initiatives to make benefits of the government programmes reach the target population better. The efforts included mobilisation of masses through public awareness campaign, ensuring the poor their rights by petitioning to government, pressurising the administration through strikes or threats of strike, and influencing the government through NGO networks.

To assess NGO impact, it was also necessary to ascertain the nature of activities pursued by NGOs. With this in view it was gathered that major activities of NGOs under rural development consisted of infrastructure work, microfinance, SHG promotion, implementation of certain components, viz., training, etc. under SGSY, training of the rural poor, employment of women in gainful activities, farm sector development, environment protection, literacy promotion, health, women and child welfare, sanitation and rural housing. As knowledge of major activities by themselves would not reveal NGOs' contribution to rural development, it required, *inter alia*, information on the scale of NGO participation and various other issues connected with NGOs. They are given in the following two paragraphs and at other places in this chapter.

Regarding NGO work under microfinance, it was gathered that participation in the matter was less than 40 per cent for NGOs, and success reported at 90 per cent credited NGOs with a good effect. Similarly, the NGOs associated with setting up of microenterprise in rural areas demonstrated encouraging results.

SHG promotion had caught the attention of many grass-roots NGOs. Grants in fact poured in from the government as well as support organisations for SHG formation, nurturing and credit linking in addition to setting of microenterprise by SHG members individually and in groups. NGOs reporting association with this kind of work were asked to state whether the programme as experienced by them was a success. The analysis showed that SHG promotion was a very popular programme, but NGOs faced difficulties in this programme due to which 31 per cent of NGOs that pursued this programme met with failure in implementation. NGOs added that making SHG a sustainable programme was the most difficult task. Due to lack of economic activities SHGs used to disintegrate after existence for a year or two, and imparting timely technical training and credit linking was the need of the hour.

During the study, technical capacity of NGOs was discussed with some respondents threadbare. It was uniformly replied by NGOs that the projects coming to them for implementation were usually less technically intensive; hence, failure rate was minimum. Further, often technical support was made available by government line departments or project sponsoring agencies. Projects were generally not underfinanced or did not suffer due to financing below the required level.

The NGO respondents were also asked as to whether they had any programme implemented for poor rural women, poor members of SC and ST communities, etc. They were also asked to name some programmes which were implemented in remote areas and its successful adoption, programmes on which money spent by NGOs compared to the government was less, and projects after completion were left to the people to manage. The NGO reply has been given hereunder:

- *Programmes for poor rural women*: Vocational training, SHG promotion, awareness creation in health/medicines, propagation of small child norm, family planning, dowry protection, relief to the disabled, assistance to the widow destitute, rural health, leprosy prevention/treatment, AIDS awareness, women empowerment, free medical check-up for pregnant women.
- *Programmes for poor SC/ST members:* Free clothing, handicrafts, health awareness, free food, disaster relief, sanitary facilities, literacy, coir work training, SHG promotion, free education to children, medical facilities.
- *Work in remote areas:* Sanitation, awareness on health, road construction and repair, vocational training, financial support to people engaged in cultivation, disaster relief, water supply, AIDS awareness, SHG promotion.
- *Programmes on Which NGOs spent less money compared to governments:* Awareness programmes, vocational training, microfinance, plantation work.
- *Projects after completion left to people to manage:* Plantation.

Autonomy is important to an NGO because it promotes freedom of function and preserves its identity. Simultaneously, NGOs have to display responsibility through an exercise of accountability to their stakeholders. Autonomy and accountability can be compared to two dissimilar pulls on an NGO in opposing directions; yet autonomy of the NGO needs to be balanced against accountability. The data generated from the study provide some important generalisations in this regard, and are given in the next few paragraphs.

NGOs did not mind losing autonomy to the government and funding agencies as long as funds kept flowing to them.

There were not many instances of NGOs losing autonomy in the past. May be, relative freedom hitherto enjoyed by NGOs was responsible for lack of concern on their part to maintain freedom. A very high majority of them also viewed that for the pursuit of their vision and mission NGOs scarcely needed to sacrifice their autonomy; thus, rural development and NGO autonomy could go together.

Despite not rating their autonomy highly, NGOs were conscious of threat potentials of agencies that closely interacted with them in their day-to-day operation. In a descending order, NGOs rated district administration as posing maximum threat to their autonomy; next, local *Panchayat* and funding agencies were indicated as potential threats. Least threatening was the state government which was generally seen as being located in the far-off state capital having remote and very subtle control over them.

The above analysis shows that NGO autonomy is not an issue with the NGOs of the district, though it has theoretical significance. NGO autonomy was a new area for the voluntary sector and the stage is not reached when its importance could be fully realised to enable NGOs to take sufficient preventive steps against dilution of NGO ideology. Relative lack of concern within NGOs for safeguarding of autonomy appeared due to the fact that they were inclined enough to work as Public Service Contractors (which are NGOs contracted to implement official programmes or components thereof). Hence, the general character of NGOs in the district looked like being that of public service contractors. This finding has important implication for the voluntary sector in particular, and the civil society in general. This will be discussed later in this chapter.

Along with autonomy another area of importance was accountability of NGOs to their stakeholders. While contracting projects from the government or international agencies, in the natural process NGOs had been accountable to them through the funders' system of reports and returns and other systems of monitoring. It was important to study accountability of NGOs to the target group/community/individuals as people were stakeholders in NGOs. This, to a large extent, has been covered later in this chapter in the paragraphs dealing with citizens' participation and perceptions by examining the extent to which NGOs succeeded in ensuring public participation in their rural development programmes.

No social actors live in a watertight environment. They necessarily work in relationships which are dynamic in nature. NGOs similarly function in an environment comprising four major relationships: NGO-government (inclusive of other state actors, viz., *Panchayat*), NGO-funders, NGO-NGO and NGO-civil society. These four relationships can determine success or failure of NGO sector in the society. It was, therefore, attempted to study NGO relationships to assess their contribution to rural development.

NGO respondents were queried about the nature of their relation with the District and Block Administration. Those who reported not-so-good or bad relationship were further queried about the reasons thereof. The respondents were also asked to categorise their relationship with the local *Panchayat* under 'good' or 'bad' categories. It was found that over 79 per cent of NGOs enjoyed good relationship with district/block administration and local *Panchayat*. A similar proportion of NGOs, as had been noticed under a preceding paragraph, also did not mind losing their autonomy for the sake of projects from the government.

The above findings, when viewed together, lead to the conclusion that the government so far had been cooperating with the NGO sector in implementation of programmes/ projects to the satisfaction of NGOs to a large extent. The sector, which was so much dependent on the government for carrying out its missions and strategy, might not do good to the autonomy of the agencies concerned, but at the moment the honeymoon in government-NGO relationship apparently contributed to the rural development. If monitoring by the government/*Panchayats* remained satisfactory, a higher degree of rural development through such partnership could be a distinct possibility in near future. It so appeared that the positive attributes of the government and voluntary sectors can be synergised to produce better results. Development cannot be a monopoly of any single sector; combination of sectors was, therefore, desirable for the sake of synergy of action and for maximum effect.

It was further noticed that a majority of NGOs were beneficiaries of the government/*Panchayat* allocated projects. Ninety per cent of NGOs were ever prepared to implement projects on behalf of the government and *Panchayat*. This finding confirmed once again the earlier finding that NGOs were largely public service contractors. The analysis also drives home the point that there had to be a proactive attempt on the part of the government to involve the NGOs which had not enjoyed government grants for implementing projects so far, in the interest of using the people's power as also participatory development in rural areas.

Questions often crossed the mind as to the degree of control of NGOs held by funding agencies by way of monitoring of projects and insisting on stiff reporting requirement which was not an easy task for satisfactory compliance. The NGO respondents was, therefore, queried whether there were instances in which funders were not satisfied with NGO-led project implementation.

It revealed from the examination of the relative data that NGOs having office infrastructure at a reasonable level did not face problem as to stringent reporting requirements of funders. Significantly, in 25 per cent of cases funding agencies were not satisfied with the quality of implementation of projects. This gave a negative outlook of NGO-led rural development. Among the reasons for funders' dissatisfaction, the following were important: lack of appropriate support from rural target people, lack of proper coordination in implementation of programmes, improper utilisation of funds, lack of knowledge regarding implementation of projects, constraints of implementation of programmes in rural areas due to absence of infrastructure, unreasonably high expectations of funders not being commensurate with funds made available under projects, non-participation of rural women in rural development at some places, mismanagement of projects, insufficient funds under certain programmes, and lack of suitable contacts which could facilitate smooth implementation of projects.

To study the relationship of the voluntary sector within itself, it was required to see the extent of NGO participation in networks, the levels at which networks functioned, and the benefits accruing to NGOs owing to networks. The analysis reveals that a huge majority of NGOs were networked at various levels. The remaining NGOs were outside the networks, in other words, operating as individual entities. Though networks were formed at block, district, state and national levels, participation at higher level NGO networks tapered off in the descending order. It implied that the highest participation was displayed at Block level, next higher level of participation was noticed at district level, a little lesser degree of participation was observed at state level, but national level participation was only a minuscule. Supplementary discussion in the matter with NGO leaders disclosed that the size of an NGO's annual budget and level of participation of the NGO in networks had a fine link. Bigger the budget, more active was the NGO in network participation at higher levels. Benefits accruing to the NGOs out of participation were also quite substantial. All NGOs were not big organisations, but synergy of these outfits was achieved, even comparable to those of big organisations, through the institution of network.

NGOs and their networks contribute immensely to the strengthening of civil society and social capital. The interaction of NGOs and the civil society is, therefore, important from the point of view of this study. In the instant case, it was presumed that the area under study contained a number of people's organisations (POs). Questions were put to NGO respondents to ascertain the expectations of NGOs from the local populace or POs, whether these expectations were met by the people or POs in course of the implementation of the programme, and the nature of assistance offered by the people/POs. Questions regarding NGO-people conflict and popular trust with NGOs were also put to NGO respondents to find the depth of relationship between the NGO and the civil society, which was vital from the point of view of programme success.

An agency working with the people should naturally have expectations from masses. It was derived from the available data that 18 per cent of NGOs had no expectations on their part from local social groups. Lack of NGO expectation from people in project area looked like being a novice talk. However, a large chunk of NGOs (69%) desired to have, among other things, moral support from the local people where projects were under implementation, and only 43 per cent of NGOs got this kind of support from the public. The large gap in two figures (26%) gave a hint as to a considerable popular apathy, possibly a resistance, to NGOs' development programmes.

This finding, when compared with two other findings, that 62 per cent of NGOs admitted that people did not trust NGOs much and that 51 per cent of NGOs did not get any assistance/support from people, confirms the observation that a considerable number of people were not well disposed to NGO activities.

Support of local social groups to the activities of NGOs was an important area to study. There was a stunning finding that 51 per cent of NGOs had no support of local social groups that further corroborated the just preceded finding that a large number of people, where projects were in operation, were not well disposed to the activities of NGOs. Further, in the interest of future of NGOs and their roles, NGO-civil society relationship had to strengthen considerably more through involvement of POs in NGO-led activities.

The issue pertaining to conflicts, if any, NGOs encountered in course of project implementation was considered very important. The study revealed that participation of people in projects implemented by NGOs often suffered from conflicts in as many as 38 per cent of cases. Had the people concerned of the projects been taken into confidence and consulted during planning of projects or implementation, the conflicts at such a high rate would not have arisen. In 23 per cent of cases conflicts had not been resolved yet, or projects were abandoned, this indicated further a lack of popular participation to that extent which appeared very high. Further, 62 per cent of NGOs did not win the people's trust so vital in social work. As 72 per cent of them reported inadequate NGO exposure to people being the reason for lack of trust, it amounted to admission on the part of NGOs that they had not worked much with the people or to the extent of earning public trust. It also means that with good amount of social work trust level can be expected to go up. The mistrust with NGOs in 28 per cent of cases was attributed to certain past activities. Such high level of mistrust could only speak ill of any organisation, let alone NGOs.

NGO respondents were asked about the benefits that the people of project areas enjoyed, pursuant to implementation of anti-poverty and other rural development programmes by them. The impact of the NGOs' anti-poverty and other rural development programmes was, however, marred by 61 NGO respondents, i.e., more than half, not preferring to answer the query. It could be that their experience had nothing positive in it to enable them to reply. However, the conclusion that was drawn was that a successful project had satisfactory impact on socio-economic condition of the target people, but project failures comprised about half the total projects or more where the target people did not have the socio-economic transformation.

Ultimately, it was important to know whether NGOs were satisfied with their role in rural development. If answer to the question was in the negative, NGO respondents were asked reasons for their dissatisfaction. The analysis showed that there was a high level of dissatisfaction prevailing among NGOs about their role in rural development. Main reasons for this dissatisfaction were unhelpful government attitude, lack of funds/projects, lack of people's involvement in programmes, lack of right kind of field staff, and, not surprisingly, failure of NGO management.

Citizen Participation and Perception

Indian official planners were conscious of the importance of the role of the pubic for the success of programmes since the beginning of planning. The First Five-Year Plan document stated that public cooperation and public opinion constituted the principal force and sanction behind planning. A democracy working for social ends had to base itself on the willing assent of the people and not the coercive power of the state. In the Second Plan, it was reiterated that public cooperation and public opinion constituted the principal force and sanction behind India's approach to planning.[32] After five decades of planning,

32. *Report of the Steering Committee on Voluntary Sector for the Tenth Five-Year Plan (2002-2007)*, Planning Commission, Government of India, January 2002, p.7.

the significance of this has not diminished; on the other hand, every programme has got oriented to generating proper public perception and solicits the target people's participation therein to ensure its success. Joel Bhose has even gone to the extent of saying that "**people's development is people's business. The essence of development is nothing but people's participation.**"[33]

According to the *Oxford English Dictionary*, to 'participate'[34] means to "share or take part". Participation thus refers to an act of sharing or taking part. Accordingly, citizens' participation connotes **act of sharing or taking part by citizens.** Parry defines it as "a process wherein people involve themselves in planning, decision making and carrying out activities, projects, movement or whatsoever towards betterment with or without external support and sustain the same as individuals, people's organisations and social institutions.... (It is) the act of taking part or having a share with others in some action."[35]

The meaning of 'perceive' as per the *Oxford English Dictionary*, is: "apprehend with mind, understand".[36] 'Perception' means "an interpretation or impression based on one's understanding of something".[37] Citizens' perception would, therefore, mean **citizens' interpretation or impression of something.**

Citizens' participation and perception of the role of NGOs would accordingly carry the following meaning: **people's sharing or taking part in and interpretation or impression of the**

---

33. Bhose, Joel S.G.R., *NGOs and Rural Development: Theory and Practice*, Concept Publishing Company, New Delhi, 2003, p.132.
34. *The Concise Oxford Dictionary of Current English,* Ninth Edition, Oxford University Press, 1995, p.996.
35. Parry, as quoted by Bhose, Joel S.G.R., *NGOs and Rural Development: Theory and Practice*, *Op. Cit.*, p.134.
36. *The Concise Oxford Dictionary of Current English, op. cit.*, pp.1013-1014.
37. *Ibid.*, p.1014.

role of NGOs. The right perception of NGOs' role by citizens carries the potential to encourage higher degree of participation of citizens in the programmes of NGOs, thereby enhancing probability of success of NGO-led initiatives. In this section, logically, the analysis centres on various perceptions generated from working of NGOs in community and the extent to which perceptions had a bearing on participation.

An organisation to undertake a project requires resources. Adequacy or otherwise of resources determines the future of the organisation's project. Where the organisation enjoys goodwill of the public, raising resources from prospective donors, to an extent, including the target people, is not considered difficult. Organisational transparency has a very important role to play in attracting donors to the cause. NGOs themselves furnished during study the position regarding contribution of various sectors to NGOs' attempt in garnering resources. In contrast, an attempt has been made here to view the citizens' perception with regard to how NGOs raised funds and their constraints.

Public awareness of NGOs' sources of funds from which they used to carry out social activities including their programmes in which people were associated, was not of very high order, as a large number of citizen respondents were not aware of the fact that the Government of India and international organisations being important sources of NGO resources. A substantial number of people did not know that NGO members' contribution to NGO funds was insufficient to carry out their mission, due to which they sought outside assistance. Transparency of NGO structure and function would demand that the people of project area as well as NGOs' vicinity knew of their strengths and weaknesses well before the NGO and people collaborated in a project. In this context, the citizens' awareness of financial standing of NGO was important.

If resources are the fuel of the engine of NGO, activities are its motion. Activities are the real measure of the effectiveness of an organisation and how citizens perceive NGO activities can to a great extent decide the degree of their participation, and, therefore, the success of the project. An elaborate analysis of NGO activities showed that the general public had a good knowledge of NGOs' nature of work, barring some instances where public awareness was lagging. The projects like microfinance, microenterprise development and SHG promotion were seen as foremost anti-poverty programmes implemented with NGO support.

NGOs, however, prefer to work for self-sustainable projects and like to hand over its management to people when they notice sufficient signs of people's capability to handle it. Development obviously aims at people's participation and gradual passing on of the control to people. The responses from citizens lead one to conclude that people lacked confidence and felt strongly deficient in their ability to manage projects independently.

The relationship of NGOs with the local government is very crucial in a developing country like India where the government is a dominant player in rural development. NGOs, therefore, have to strike a proper balance with the government. The type and quality of relationship is determined by missions and strategies of NGOs concerned. While NGOs strive to maintain a relationship according to the organisational need, citizens' perception of the relationship as well as its impact on them contributes to either enhancing or reducing the faith and confidence reposed by them in the NGOs. This, in final analysis, is the central element in citizens' participation. The data in this respect revealed that the people perceived NGOs' relationship with the administration and local *Panchayat* as generally cordial; wherever there was poor relationship with the government, it was mostly due to the absence of proper attitude conducive to good relations with NGOs from the side of the government. A vast majority of citizens wished that people's developmental issues should be taken up by NGOs with the government for redressal.

Proliferation of NGOs and their greater role in development activities *vis-à-vis* government's original role had put a question as to whose implementation of rural development programme was better. The citizens' perception regarding implementation of rural development projects was tilted in favour NGOs than the government.

NGO-civil society relation is as much important as NGO-government relation. The former has a direct bearing on citizens' participation in NGO-led projects. It is, therefore, important to study the major aspect of this relation, i.e., conflict in NGO-people relation. According to the perception of nine-tenth of citizen respondents, there were no conflicts, or conflicts whenever arose got resolved amicably, which implied that NGO-civil society relationship on the average, was, cordial, but irritants reported, to the tune of remaining tenth, that it should have been avoided through consultation of citizens during project formation, or well before the start of the projects in the interest of higher level of public participation.

Citizen respondents, in this connection, were asked whether people were consulted during project formulation and implementation. Further, they were prompted for responses on a query whether people concerned with the projects implemented by NGOs participated in the projects; if not, reasons for nonparticipation thereof. The clear conclusion coming from the data received was that NGOs had not done enough to mobilise full participation from people in their programmes. NGO efforts were often limited to meeting the leaders of the community and expecting them to solicit participation from the project people. No wonder participation touched only 57 per cent level which was not enough for success of any programme. NGOs' pre-programme consultation did not register a very high point, i.e., 63 per cent, which required to improve substantially more to push through development programmes with target communities.

Related to consultation and participation was support/ services provided by people to NGOs in the project areas which were examined next. It was found that 48 per cent of people did not provide any assistance/support to NGOs working for their community. Thus, NGOs had a tough time with people, and they had to go a long way to ensure full participation or involvement. Why did NGOs not receive full participation from masses? Maybe, the answer to this lies in the citizens' perception of the benefactors, i.e., NGOs. The question relating to citizen respondents' ratings of integrity of NGOs was revealing. It came to light that a majority did not hold a good opinion of NGO integrity and to about 14 per cent the NGOs' integrity was shrouded in mystery. Apparently, NGOs had to do a lot to improve their image in public.

A similar question was put in the questionnaire for citizen respondents. It was asked whether citizen respondents trusted NGOs; if not, the reasons thereof. The responses received were worth comparing to either confirm or adjust results in regard to NGOs' integrity. The results of the analysis in this regard more or less coincided with the finding that NGOs had to work harder to improve their image with the public. Low level of trust could not encourage the public to participate in projects.

What were the benefits accruing to the people from NGOs' anti-poverty or rural development programmes? This was necessary for our assessment because without the first-hand information as to how NGO programmes performed, their contribution to rural development could not be estimated. Further, higher level of participation demanded that the message about benefits secured by the participating people should circulate among all so that the people with lesser awareness and participation would come forward for change in their fortune. People's material conditions had apparently improved with programmes implemented by NGOs, but inability of a vast number of NGO respondents (discussed a little earlier) to indicate the benefits brought a degree of uncertainty to the observations of citizen respondents. However, the clear and unambiguous answers as to benefits to the people added strength to the idea that anti-poverty and rural development programmes had their impact. With increased participation the result was bound to be better.

Last but not least, whether citizen respondents were satisfied with NGO performance? What were the reasons for NGOs' poor performance? It was found that a substantial majority of citizen respondents, i.e., at over 62 per cent, was satisfied with NGO performance in rural development in general. Satisfaction of citizen respondents at that level was reasonable, and with improvement in people's trust and perception of NGOs' integrity, it could be hoped that NGOs would satisfy fully the rural population in their search for development. Nonetheless, the reasons given for NGO failure (albeit by a small proportion of NGO respondents), such as NGOs as institutions not capable and failure of the NGO management, were devastating to the NGO cause.

11

People's Programme: A New Approach to Poverty Removal

> *Good governance removes poverty and ushers in prosperity. During bad governance, which leads to corruption and inefficiency, you need to change strategy for removal of poverty so that poverty eradication as an objective is achieved. The sad fact is that there is no effective strategy to remove poverty where governance is corrupt.*
>
> – ***Author's reflection***

India has experimented since Independence many approaches to removal of poverty in the country. Most of the approaches involved government-centred programmes, which resulted in failure or success less than at desired levels. Efforts to involve public participation in a very few cases have succeeded, depending upon personal contribution from implementers of the programmes. India, with its 300 million poor, needs a sound strategy to remove poverty in a mass scale.

During the course of study, certain finer points regarding the working of voluntary, government and business sectors were noticed which have been developed in this chapter to construct a new, model approach for removal of poverty. In this approach, the target people have occupied the centre stage. It is an approach supposed to be implemented by the people for themselves. Hence, the title – People's Programme. Though the programme has been worked out in some detail for poverty removal activity, it can well apply to rural development with necessary modifications.

Current Strategy

In the Tenth Five-Year Plan, the government has adopted mainly the strategy of organising the poor as Self-Help Groups (SHGs) for implementation of its anti-poverty programmes. The SHG programme is an improvisation over earlier anti-poverty and income generation programmes in that it mobilises the hitherto unknown group dynamics in attaining economic welfare by the poor. Starting from formation of SHG to taking up of economic activities, SHG is self-propelled. The job of the government mostly lies in guidance and creating facilities/infrastructure for the upcoming groups for their effective absorption into the economic mainstream.

In the scheme of things under discussion, NGOs have been given a very important role. They organise groups, nurture them, and finally help them get linked up with financing agencies for production and marketing of goods and services. From the stage of formation of groups to marketing of SHG products, in innumerable cases, NGOs have given the much needed support, i.e., backward and forward linkage, to SHGs enabling them to survive and compete in the free market economy. Thus, NGOs have worked as catalysts for economic change (due to their decentralised structure, absence of hierarchy and enough scope within the organisation for innovation) and work for rural development better than their rival, i.e., the government. The objective of this chapter is to propound a system in the existing anti-poverty programmes by which the role of NGO can get more serious and vigorous to significantly improve the impact of the poverty alleviation scenario in the country.

Theory of Influence

In the background of successful voluntary efforts spread over the length and breadth of the country and the essential role of the government and the business sector in modern day economy, the role of **a threesome force** in the socio-economic life of a community is generally observed. The three forces are **authority** (that stands for the government), **voluntarism** (representing the power of the civil society), and (motive of) **profit** (which is the moving force behind business). It is presumed that programmes designed to work in the social system, without integrating all the above three forces, would not succeed fully. The current approach, therefore, synthesises the government sector (or programme sponsoring agency) with the NGO and business sectors with regard to their main principles.

Modus Operandi of People's Programme

The following paragraphs chart out the programme in conformity with the theory of the three forces.

The approach envisages that there will be NGOs working for anti-poverty programmes among people. They must be drafted after a rigorous test of their credentials and assigned 20/30 families/individuals/individuals in groups in a year for a period of five to seven years. The NGOs would provide consultancy, training and backward and forward linkages to the families/persons allotted to them. Every year, the NGOs may be free to add 20/30 families/individuals to their project portfolio.

Normally, the programmes of the government and other agencies do have a component to meet NGOs' administrative expenses, but it is proposed to devise additionally a scheme of incentives for NGOs who succeed in lifting the poor below the poverty line at least to a pre-determined level of sufficiency and prosperity. The incentive should be available only after due examination of pre-programme and post-programme economic status of families/individuals/individuals in groups, certificate for which has to be ensured from local *Panchayat* and/or Block authorities.

Since economic stabilisation of the poor comes only over a period of about five years or more, the incentive should be payable only after five years after observing the success of raising the poor above the poverty line. Hence, in case each year an NGO takes up 20/30 families/individuals for a period of five years, the NGO shall be entitled to claim incentive after five years from the programme sponsoring agency. Considering the effort involved in the task of implementing the programmes in rural areas, Rs. 2 to 3 lakh incentives per family or individual to the associated NGO after successful implementation of the programme would not be considered unreasonable. Thus, it is tried to dovetail the principle of business, i.e., *profit*, favourably in the working of *voluntarism* and *authority* in society in recognition of the desire of every man to profit from his activity.

On an average, 30 crore poor in India, if raised above poverty line, should incur an expenditure by way of incentives to the tune of Rs. 6000 to 9000 crore over a period of five years or more, which is certainly a small amount considering the size of budgets of present day governments and the prospect and spin-off effect of ushering in the poor in to the economic reckoning or money economy.

From the NGO point of view, about Rs. 50 lakh income as incentive every year after five or seven years of successful programme implementation is substantial. The proposed incentive is supposed to provide enough enthusiasm to NGOs to put in extra efforts necessary to show positive results in the field. Hence, there exists a win-win scenario for all concerned, i.e., the government, the NGO, and the poor. Nevertheless, the programme sponsoring agency has to ensure a few things for success of incentive-based programmes. The programme should operate on project basis, i.e., NGOs have to submit a detailed proposal along with families/individuals/individuals in groups proposed including record of their pre-development socio-economic condition, which on thorough scrutiny by the *Panchayat* and/or block authorities, should be given the signal to go ahead.

Basis to Judge Success of Programme

At the time an NGO claims incentive, the following parameters should form the basis for examining the success of the families/individuals/individuals in groups crossing the poverty line:

- Income is sufficient to declare the beneficiary way above (to be decided as a policy) the official poverty line.
- Income of the beneficiary is sustainable over a period of time, say for five or seven years (to be documented by the NGO sponsoring the beneficiary and supported by *Panchayat*/ Block authorities).
- The children in the family of a beneficiary attend school and those above 10 years of age have acquired the skill of reading and writing.
- The beneficiary under the charge of NGO has a better (say at least a tiled) house.
- The family of the beneficiary has its own source of drinking water.
- The family of the beneficiary has a sanitary toilet.

Annexures

ANNEXURE I

Summary of Government of India Policy towards Voluntary Sector[1]

The voluntary sector has been given due importance in the planning process right from the **First Five-Year Plan**, as emphasis was given on public cooperation in national development with the help of VOs. It was highlighted in the First Plan document that the "Public cooperation and public opinion constitute the principal force and sanction behind planning. A democracy working for social ends has to base itself on the willing assent of the people and not the coercive power of the State." In the **Second Plan**, it was reiterated that public cooperation and public opinion constitute the principal force and sanction behind India's approach to planning. It was observed that wherever the people, especially in rural areas, have been approached, they have responded with eagerness. In national extension and community project areas, in local development works, in *shramdaan*, in social welfare extension projects and in

1. Collected from *Report of the Steering Committee on Voluntary Sector for the Tenth Five-Year Plan (2002-2007)*, Planning Commission, Government of India, January 2002, pp.34-39.

the work of voluntary organisations, there has always been willingness and enthusiasm on the part of the people to contribute in terms of labour, and local resources have been made freely available.

The **Third Five-Year Plan** emphasised that "The concept of public cooperation is related to the much larger sphere of voluntary action in which the initiative and organisational responsibility rest completely with the people and their leaders, and does not rely on legal sanctions or the power of the State for achieving its aims. It was realised that so vast are the unsatisfied needs of the people that all the investments in the public and private sectors together can only make a limited provision for them. Properly organised voluntary effort may go for towards augmenting the facilities available to the community for helping the weakest to a somewhat better life. The wherewithal for this has to come from time, energy and other resources of millions of people for whom VOs can find constructive channels suited to the varying conditions in the country." During the **Fourth** and **Fifth Plans**, the thrust on public cooperation and involvement of people's organisation was lost due to attack on over territory and recession that followed. During this period investment was focussed especially in intensive agricultural programmes.

In the **Sixth Five-Year Plan**, the idea of participation of people's organisations was again recognised. Success stories in the field, of VOs like the Jamkhed Project on child and health care in Maharashtra, Bharat Agro Industries Foundation's work in animal husbandry, and social forestry and Self-Employed Women's Association (SEWA) were quoted and it was stated that the country is dotted with numerous examples of highly successful voluntary action of this nature.

Role of VOs in development got a further fillip in the **Seventh Five-Year Plan** where it was declared that serious efforts would be made to involve VOs in various development programmes to supplement the government efforts to offer the rural poor choices and alternatives. The emphasis continued till the ongoing Ninth Plan, wherein efforts are being made to promote peoples' participatory bodies like *Panchayati Raj* Institutions (PRIs), Self-help Groups and NGOs for development. The following criteria were identified for identifying voluntary agencies for enlisting help in relation to the rural development programmes:

- The organisation should be a legal entity.
- It should be based in a rural area and be working there for a minimum of three years.
- It should have broad-based objectives serving the social and economic needs of the community as a whole and mainly the weaker sections. It must not work for profit but on 'no profit and no loss' basis.
- Its activities should be open to all citizens of India irrespective of religion, caste, creed, sex or race.
- It should have the necessary flexibility, professional competence and organisational skills to implement programmes.
- Its office bearers should not be elected members of any political party.
- It declares that it will adopt constitutional and non-violent means for rural development purposes.
- It is committed to secular and democratic concepts and methods of functioning.

In the **Eighth Plan** document, due emphasis was given on building up people's institutions. It was admitted that developmental activities undertaken with people's active participation have a greater chance of success, and can also be more cost-effective as compared to the development activities undertaken by the government where people become passive observers. It was admitted that a lot in the area of education (especially literacy), health, family planning, land improvement, efficient land use, minor irrigation, watershed management, recovery of wastelands, a forestation, animal husbandry, dairy, fisheries and sericulture etc. could be achieved by creating people's institutions accountable to the community. Therefore the focus of attention will be on developing multiple institutional options for improving the delivery systems by using the vast potential of the voluntary sector.

In the **Ninth Five-Year Plan**, it was admitted that private initiative, whether individual collective or community based, forms the essence the development strategy articulated in the Plan, and efforts to be made to remove disadvantages which had prevented some segments of our society in participating effectively in the development process. Keeping up with this line of thinking, "promoting and developing people's participatory bodies like Panchayati Raj Institutions, cooperatives and self-help groups" was one of the objectives of the Ninth Plan.

The Mid-Term Review (MTR) of the Ninth Five-Year Plan (October 2000) has also documented some successful and sustainable projects undertaken by VOs and other people's organisations. The MTR has identified following problems in the performance of Central and State Plans. Some of these problems faced by the country can be mitigated by the emerging voluntary sector as a compliment and supplement to the State efforts.

- The critical factor appears to be effective governance to ensure balanced growth of the different regions of India.
- Development is an outcome of efficient institutions rather than the other way around. There is a need to focus on building institutions and improving governance from maximising the quantity of development funding to maximising of development outcomes and effectiveness and efficiency of public service delivery.

Further, under the 'Directions for Reforms' of MTR, it has been *inter alia* suggested that "Initiatives by local bodies, NGOs and women need to be encouraged", to resolve some of the problems referred to above.

It has been observed in the Approach Paper to the **Tenth Plan** that in many states, we have: hospitals/dispensaries but absence of personnel and there are school buildings but teachers do not show up. To rectify these anomalies and to achieve most of the targets set up for the Tenth Plan, the need to promote voluntary sector has been recognised. The theme of encouragement to voluntary sector continued in the Approach Paper to the Tenth Plan, and is reflected in the following words, "In view of the continued importance of public action in our development process, increasing the efficiency of public interventions must also take high priority". The minimum agenda proposed in the Approach Paper has recognised voluntary sector by putting "greater decentralisation to PRIs and other people's organisations" as one of the items for the Tenth Plan.

The voluntary sector deserves encouragement to ameliorate at least some of the above problems, because of its following comparative advantages:

- VOs/NGOs are much closer to the poorer and disadvantaged sections of the society.
- Staff of VOs is normally highly motivated and altruistic in behaviour.
- VOs can easily stimulate and mobilise community resources and have access to volunteers.
- They are more effective in bringing people's participation.
- VOs are less rule-bound and are non-bureaucratic, non-formal and flexible in their structure and operations.
- Voluntary sector has greater potential for innovations.
- VOs prefer to work in a multi-sectoral framework.
- VOs are catalysts for creating social cohesion (Kumar 1998).

Certain disadvantages or shortcomings of voluntary sector are also well-known, namely, their inability to cooperate with each other in a way which would allow for coherent policy making, their accountability and transparency is not perfect and their operations are smaller in scale. Therefore, there is a need to improvise the working of VOs by scaling up their operations and by making them transparent and accountable.

ANNEXURE II
Important Rural Development Initiatives during Five-Year Plans[2]

First Five-Year Plan 1951-56:

- Bhoodan Movement, 1951.
- Gramdan Movement, 1952.
- Community Development Programme, 1952.
- National Agricultural Extension Service, 1953.

Second Five-Year Plan 1956-61:

- Khadi and Village Industries Programme, 1957.
- Village Housing Projects Scheme, 1957.
- Panchayati Raj, 1959.
- Multi-purpose Tribal Development Blocks Programme, 1959.
- Package Programme, 1960.
- Intensive Agriculture District Programme, 1960.

Third Five-Year Plan 1961-66:

- Tribal Area Development Programme, 1962.
- Hill Area Development Programme, 1962.

---

2. **Sources**: Bhose, Joel S.G.R., *NGOs and Rural Development: Theory and Practice,* Concept Publishing Company, New Delhi, 2003, pp.71-73.

   Maheswari, S.R., *Rural Development in India: A Public Policy Approach,* Sage Publications, New Delhi, 1985, pp.30-34.

   Singh, Abha Lakshmi and Fazal, Shahab, *Agriculture and Rural Development,* B.R. Publishing Corporation, Delhi 1998, pp.24-59.

   www.indianembassy.org (Chapter 17)

   www.rural.nic.in

   Repetition of programme names in this list under different five year plans implies that the programmes finding mention under different five-year plans are continued or revived from earlier plan/s with or without changes.

- Rural Industrial Project, 1962.
- Applied Nutrition Programme, 1962.
- Intensive Agricultural Area Programme, 1964.
- Intensive Area Development Scheme, 1965.
- High-Yielding Variety Programme, 1965.

Three Annual Plans 1966-69:

- Farmers Training and Education Programme, 1966.
- Well Construction Programme, 1966.
- Rural Works Programme, 1967.
- Tribal Development Block, 1968.
- Rural Manpower Programme, 1969.
- Agency for Development of Marginal Farmers and Agricultural Labourers,[3] 1969.

Fourth Five-Year Plan 1969-74:

- Drought Prone Area Programme, 1970.
- Small Farmers' Development Agency,[4] 1971.
- Rural Works Programme, 1971.
- Crash Scheme for Rural Employment, 1971.
- Tribal Area Development Programme, 1972.
- Pilot Project for Tribal Development, 1972.
- Pilot Intensive Rural Employment Projects, 1972.

Fifth Five-Year Plan 1974-79:

- Command Area Development Programme, 1974.

---

3. Started as a separate programme, later merged to Small Farmers' Development Programme.
4. Merged to IRD Programme and subsequently to SGSY.

- Minimum Needs Programme,[5] 1974.
- Twenty Point Programme, 1975.
- Special Livestock Production Programme, 1975.
- Habitat Movement, 1976.
- Rural Functional Literacy Programme, 1976.
- Food for Work Programme,[6] 1977.
- Antyodaya,[7] 1977.
- Desert Development Programme, 1977.
- Comprehensive Area Development Programme, 1978.
- District Industries Centre, 1978.
- Operation Barga, 1978.
- Integrated Rural Development Programme, 1979.
- Training of Rural Youth or Self-Employment, 1979.
- National Adult Education Programme, 1979.
- Whole Village Development Programme, 1979.

Sixth Five-Year Plan 1980-85:

- National Rural Employment Programme,[8] 1980.
- Prime Minister's New 20-Point Programme, 1980.
- Biogas Programme, 1981.
- Development of Women and Children in Rural Areas, 1983.

---

5. Elementary education, rural health, rural water supply, rural roads, rural electrification, housing assistance to rural landless labourers, environmental improvement of urban slums and nutrition constitute the ingredients of the programme.
6. Commenced during the Fifth Plan (1974-79) and continued since then.
7. It is a Gandhian programme to uplift 'the last man in the row.' See Mathur, B.L., *Rural Development and Cooperation*, RBSA Publishers, Jaipur, 1996, p.61.
8. Started in 1975 and revised in 1982 as New 20-Point Programme.

- Rural Landless Employment Guarantee Programme, 1983.
- Self-Employment to Educated Unemployed Youth Programme, 1983.
- Employment Guarantee Programme, 1983.
- Special Programmes for Women and Children.
- Programmes for Depressed Areas.
- National Seeds Programme.
- Village and Small Industries Programme.
- Dairy Development Programme.
- Tribal Development Agency.
- Intensive Pulses Development Programme.
- Summer Moong Production Programme.
- Intensive Cotton Development Programme.
- Khadi and Village Industries Programme.

Seventh Five-Year Plan 1985-90:

- Community Development Programme.
- Integrated Rural Development Programme.
- Drought Prone Area Programme.
- Integrated Rural Energy Planning Programme.
- Desert Development Programme.
- Border Areas Development Programme.
- Command Area Development Programme.
- Biogas Development Programme.
- Social Welfare Strategy.
- Planning for Development of Village Programme.
- Rural Sanitation Programme, 1986.
- National Drinking Water Mission, 1986.
- Forest Farming for Rural Poor, 1986.
- Indira Awaas Yojna, 1986.

- Jawahar Rojgar Yojna, 1989.

Eighth Five-Year Plan 1992-97:

- Crop Production Oriented Programmes.
- Rajiv Gandhi National Drinking Water Mission, 1991.
- Animal Husbandry and Dairy Development Programme.
- Employment Assurance Scheme, 1993.
- Family Credit Plan, 1993.
- Technology Development Extension and Training, 1993.
- Investment Promotion Scheme, 1994.
- National Social Assistance Programme, 1995.
- Integrated Wastelands Development Programme, 1995.
- Agricultural Research and Education Programme.
- National Watershed Development Programme, 1996.
- Centrally Sponsored Rural Sanitation Programme.

Ninth Five-Year Plan 1997-02:

- 73rd Amendment Act of 1992 on Panchayati Raj.[9]
- Jawahar Gram Samridhi Yojna, 1999.
- Employment Assurance Scheme, 1999.
- Rajiv Gandhi National Drinking Water Mission.
- Indira Awaas Yojna.
- Centrally Sponsored Rural Sanitation Programme.
- Drought Prone Area Programme.
- Desert Development Programme.
- Integrated Wastelands Development Programme.
- Innovative Stream for Rural Housing and Habitat Development, 1999.

---

9. Came into effect in 1993.

- Agricultural Insurance Scheme, 1999.
- Swarnajayanti Gram Swarojgar Yojna, 1999.

Tenth Five-Year Plan 2002-07:

- Pradhan Mantri Gram Sadak Yojna.
- Swarnajayanti Gram Swarojgar Yojna.
- Sampoorna Grameen Rozgar Yojna.
- Indira Awaas Yojna.
- National Social Assistance Programme.
- Accelerated Rural Water Supply Programme.
- Centrally Sponsored Rural Sanitation Programme.
- Integrated Wasteland Development Project Scheme.
- Drought Prone Area Programme.
- Desert Development Programme.
- Technology Development Extension and Training.
- Investment Promotion Scheme.
- National Rural Employment Guarantee Act, 2004.

ANNEXURE III
List of Schemes of Government of India for Assistance to NGOs[10]

Ministry of Human Resources Development

Department of Women and Child Development

1. Support to Training and Employment Programme (STEP).
2. Setting up of Employment and Income Generating Training-cum-Production Units for Women (NORAD).
3. Construction/Expansion of Hostel Building for Working Women with a Day Care Centre.
4. Short Stay Homes for Women and Girls (SSH).
5. Education Work for Prevention of Atrocities on Women.
6. Balika Samriddhi Yojana (BSY).
7. National Crèche Fund Scheme 1994.
8. General Grant-in-aid for Voluntary Organisations in the field of Women and Child Development.
9. Organisational Assistance to Voluntary Organisations for Women and Child Development.
10. Grant-in-aid for Research and Publications.

National Institute of Public Cooperation and Child Development (NIPCCD)

11. National Children's Fund (NCF).

Central Social Welfare Board (CSWB)

12. Awareness Generation Programme (AGP).
13. Condensed Courses of Education for Women.

---

10. *Report of the Steering Committee on Voluntary Sector for the Tenth Five-Year Plan (2002-2007)*, Planning Commission, Government of India, January 2002, pp.34-39.

14. Socio-Economic Programme (SEP).
15. Family Counselling Centres.
16. Working Women's Hostels.
17. Crèches/Day Care Centers for Children of working/ailing mothers.

Rashtriya Mahila Kosh

18. Main Loan Scheme of Rashtriya Mahila Kosh.
19. Loan Promotion Scheme.
20. Revolving Fund Scheme.
21. Scheme for Development and Stabilisation of Self-Help Groups.
22. Death Relief and Rehabilitation Fund Scheme.
23. Nodal Agency Scheme.
24. Marketing Finance Scheme.

Ministry of Rural Development

Council for Advancement of People's Action and Rural Technology (CAPART)

1. Promotion of Voluntary Action in Rural Development (Public Cooperation Scheme).
2. Organisation of Beneficiaries Scheme.
3. Watershed Conservation and Development Programme.
4. Advancement of Rural Technology Scheme.
5. Disability – A strategy to promote the participation of people with Disabilities in programmes for Rural Development.

Department of Rural Development

1. Swarnjayanti Gram Swarozgar Yojana.

2. Innovative stream for Rural Housing and Habitat Development Scheme.
3. Scheme of rural Building Centres.
4. Credit-cum-Subsidy Scheme for Rural Housing.
5. National Social Assistance Programme.
6. Samagra Awaas Yojana.
7. Indira Awaas Yojana.

Department of Land Resources

1. Integrated Wastelands Development Project (IWDP).
2. Technology Development, Extension and Training Scheme for Wasteland Development in Non-forest Areas.
3. Investment Promotional Scheme for Development of Non-forest Wastelands.
4. Grants-in-aid to NGOs/VAs for undertaking works relating to Afforestation and Wasteland Development.

Department of Drinking Water

1. Accelerated Rural Water Supply Programme.
2. Central Rural Sanitation Programme.

Ministry of Health and Family Welfare

Department of Family Welfare

1. Scheme of Reproductive and Child Health.
2. Sterilisation Bed Scheme.
3. Urban Revamping Scheme.
4. Scheme of Multipurpose Female Health Workers ANMs Training Programme.
5. Grant-in-aid under Standing Committee on Voluntary Action.
6. Social Marketing Scheme.

Department of Health

1. Scheme of Improvement of Medical Services.
2. Scheme for Promotion and Development of Voluntary Blood Donation Programme.
3. Special Health Scheme for Rural Areas.
4. Scheme of National Anti-Malaria Programme.
5. Scheme for financial assistance to VOs for undertaking Leprosy Survey, Education and Treatment.
6. Scheme for Treatment of Tuberculosis.
7. Scheme for Control of Blindness.
8. Scheme for Control of AIDS.
9. Scheme for Undertaking Health Education and Early Detection Activities in Cancer.
10. Scheme for financial assistance to Voluntary Organisations for setting up of Cobalt Therapy Units.
11. Scheme for Prevention of Food Adulteration.
12. Scheme for Assistance to Voluntary Organisations under Drug De-addiction Programme.
13. Scheme for Opening of Schools of Nursing.
14. Scheme for Grant-in-aid to NGOs for Setting up or Expansion of Eye Care Units in Tribal/Remote Areas.
15. Scheme for Voluntary Organisations Setting up Book Banks for SC/ST Students.
16. Grant-in-aid to VOs to Undertake Sample Survey/Research on Areas of Public Health, Problems/Diseases.

Department of Indian Systems of Medicine and Homeopathy

1. Scheme for Re-orientation Training programme of ISM&H Personnel.
2. Scheme of Information Education and Communication.
3. Scheme for International Exchange Programme/Seminar/Workshops in ISM&H.

4. Scheme of Extra-Mural Research on Indian Systems of Medicine and Homeopathy.
5. Scheme of Indian Systems of Medicine in Reproduction and Child Health Programme.

Ministry of Tribal Affairs

1. Scheme of Grant-in-Aid to Voluntary Organisation Working for the Welfare of Scheduled Tribes.
2. Schemes of Educational Complex in Low Literacy Pockets for Development of Girls Literacy in Tribal Areas.
3. Scheme of Vocational Training Centre in Tribal Areas.
4. Scheme of Financial Assistance to Voluntary Organisations for Development of Primitive Tribal Groups.
5. Scheme of Grant-in-Aid to VOs for Supporting Research and Evaluation/Workshop/Seminars and Publication projects of all Indian or Inter-State Nature.

Ministry of Social Justice and Empowerment

Scheduled Castes Development Programmes

1. National Scheme of Liberation and Rehabilitation of Scavengers and their Dependents.
2. National Scheduled Castes and Scheduled Tribes Finance and Development Corporation.
3. Scheme of Special Educational Development Programme for Scheduled Castes Girls belonging to very Low literacy levels.
4. Scheme of Construction of Hostel Buildings for Scheduled Caste Boys and Girls.
5. Coaching and Allied Scheme for Scheduled Caste and Scheduled Tribe Students.
6. Scheme of Financial Assistance to Voluntary Organisations for Supporting Projects of All India or Inter-State nature for Scheduled Caste Development.

7. Grant-in-Aid to Voluntary Organisations working for the Development of Scheduled Castes.

Development Programmes of Other Backward Classes

8. Scheme of Construction of Hostel for other backward class boys and girls.
9. Scheme of Pre-examination Coaching for Other Backward Classes (OBCs).
10. Scheme of Assistance to Voluntary Organisations for the Welfare of OBCs.
11. Financial Assistance under National Backward Classes Finance and Development Corporation Development Programmes for the Minorities.
12. Scheme of Pre-examination Coaching for Weaker Sections Among Minorities based on Economic Criteria.
13. Scheme of Financial Assistance under National Minorities Development and Finance Corporation.
    13.1 Scheme of Micro-Financing to Minorities through NGOs.
14. Maulana Azad Education Foundation's Grant-in-Aid to Voluntary organisations.
    14.1 Scheme of Financial Assistance to Voluntary Organisations to establish School/Residential School mainly for Girls.
    14.2 Scheme of Financial Assistance to Voluntary Organisations to Technical/Professional Institutions.
15. Central Wakf Council's Grants to Wakf Boards/Wakf institution for development of Urban Wakf Properties.
    15.1 Scheme of Financial Assistance for the Development of Urban Wakf properties.
    15.2 Scheme of Financial Assistance to Wakf Institutions for Educational Development Programmes for Welfare of Persons with Disabilities.

16. Scheme to Promote Voluntary Action for Persons with Disabilities.
17. Scheme of Assistance to Disabled Persons for Purchase/Fitting of Aids and Appliances.
18. Scheme of Financial Assistance to NGOs under Science and Technology Project in Mission Mode on Application of Technology for the Welfare of the Handicapped.
19. Scheme of Assistance under National Handicapped Finance and Development Corporation.
    19.1 Financial Assistance to Disabled Persons through Micro Financing Scheme.
20. National Trust Fund Scheme for the Welfare of Persons with Autism, Cerebral Palsy, Mental Retardation and Multiple Disability, Social Defence Programmes, Programmes for Older Persons.
21. Scheme for Integrated Programme for Older Persons.
22. Scheme of Assistance to Panchayati Raj Institutions/ Voluntary Organisations/Self-Help Groups for Construction of Old Age Homes/Multi-Service Centres for Older Persons Programmes for Children.
23. Schemes of Integrated Programme for Street Children.
24. Scheme of Juvenile Justice.
25. Scheme of Grant-in-Aid to Homes for infants (Shishu Greh) in Promoting In-Country Adoption Programme for Prevention of Alcoholism and Substance (Drugs) Abuse.
26. Scheme for Prevention of Alcoholism and Substance (Drugs) Abuse Other Social Defence Programme.
27. Scheme of Assistance to Voluntary Organisations for Providing social Defence Services Social Welfare Research/ Evaluation and publication.
28. Scheme of Grant-in-Aid for Social Welfare Research/Evaluation and Publication.

Ministry of Environment and Forest

Eco-Regeneration and Development Programme

1. Grant-in-aid Scheme for Voluntary Organisations.
2. Scheme of Eco-Development Camps.
3. Scheme of National Environmental Awareness Campaign.
4. Scheme of Financial Assistance to VOs for Setting up Eco-clubs in schools.
5. Scheme of Environment Education in schools.
6. Scheme of Assistance for Seminars/Symposia/Workshops on Environment.
7. Scheme of Environment Information System.

Environmental Research and Development Programme

1. Man and Biosphere Programme.
2. Programme on Biosphere Reserves.
3. Programme on Wetlands.
4. Programme on Mangroves.
5. Programme on Coral Reefs.
6. Scheme of National Natural Resource Management System.

Department of Science and Technology

Science and Society Programme

1. Science and Technology for Rural Development.
2. Science and Technology for Women.
3. Science and Technology for Weaker Section.
4. Special Component Plan Scheme of Science and Technology for the Development of Scheduled Castes.
5. Science and Technology for Tribal Development (Tribal Sub-Plan).

6. Scheme for Young Scientists Scientific Research Programme.
7. Scheme of Utilisation of Scientific Expertise of Retired Scientists, Science and Technology Communication and Popularisation Programme.
8. Programme of Training in S&T Communication.
9. Voluntary Blood Donation Programme.
10. S&T Communication Software Development.
11. Research in S&T Communication.
12. Field Programmes.
13. Projects with Emphasis on Specific Areas.

Department of Culture

1. Building and equipment grants to voluntary cultural organisations.
2. Grants in aid to Voluntary Organisations/Societies for development and maintenance of National Memorials.
3. Promotion and strengthening of Regional and Local Museums.
4. Preservation and development of the cultural heritage of the Himalayas.
5. Promotion and dissemination of tribal/folk art and culture
6. Development of Buddhist-Tibetan culture and art.
7. Financial assistance for research support to Voluntary Organisations engaged in cultural activities.
8. Financial assistance to voluntary organisations for celebration of centenaries of important personalities.

ANNEXURE IV
Method of Study

An empirical method was adopted for the study. For the purpose of collecting primary data, two sets of questionnaires were circulated among sample respondents – pertaining to NGOs and citizens. The data so collected were supplemented through personal interviews of the respondents and others concerned with the research. Information and data were also collected from published as well as unpublished books, official records, and other available documents for verification of the foregoing hypotheses.

Sample and Coverage

There are 11 Blocks spread over 7 Tahasils in Puri district. Of the 11 Blocks, 10 per cent, i.e., one Block, viz. Puri Sadar, was selected for in depth study. Puri Sadar being a rural area the NGOs serving the region were mostly having their administrative offices at the nearest town, Puri. As per the *Directory of Voluntary Organisations, Orissa – 2004* published by PDC-Network, Bhubaneswar, there are 248 NGOs in the district, engaged in rural development, of which 10 per cent, i.e., 25 NGOs were selected on random basis subject to the condition that they should have some rural development programme/s run or running for sufficiently long time in Puri Sadar region. Four or five leaders/office-bearers of every selected NGO were given a questionnaire, each earmarked for NGO respondents. Thus, duly filled in questionnaires were collected from 120 NGO respondents. To study citizens' participation and perception, 5 out of 95 census villages were selected at random subject, however, to the condition that one village should have population above 2,000, two villages should have population between 1,000 and 2,000, the remaining between 500 and 1,000, and the villages should have been referred to by sample

NGOs for having implemented or implementing programme/s contributing to rural development of the area concerned. From villages having a population below 1,000, a total of 42 responses equally shared by them were collected, and the remaining three villages contributed 27 responses each. Thus, a total of 123 responses were collected from five select villages with varying importance owing to differing size of population, but the number of samples was sufficiently large for each village so as to cancel out error, if any, in observations of the citizen respondents. It was also tried to be ensured that 50 per cent of the respondents should belong to the poor strata deserving attention of NGOs having association with any of their rural development projects.

Overview of Sample Villages

There are 95 census villages in Sadar sub-district in respect of which socio-economic data from Census of India 2001 are available. For the purpose of study, five villages were selected on preliminary examination of their socio-economic parameters, size of population and NGO involvement in rural development work. The names of the villages are: Arada, Gadabhinguara, Harekrushnapur, Redhagarg and Rendua.

While the total population of the villages stood at 749, 1,548, 2,344, 818 and 1,146 respectively, the number of households ranged between 138 and 461. The proportions of S.C. population in respect of the villages were 10.3, 23.4, 37.3, 9.2 and 11.6 (in this order). Literacy/illiteracy rates for the villages in question were 81.0/31.3, 74.6/37.2, 69.9/42.7, 82.4/29.8 and 78.3/29.3 respectively. The proportions of people depending on agriculture in respect of the villages were 86.0, 82.6, 42.4, 74.5 and 73.5 (in this order). Thus, the analysis shows that the villages chosen for study did hardly have features demonstrating development of the people and needed support by way of intensive rural development programmes.

Techniques of Data Collection

In order to collect data every sample respondent, both from NGOs and citizens, was met personally and the questionnaires were filled in with the answers by them and was interviewed. Where no answer was available from a respondent, another person fulfilling the criteria was sought and answer was sought from the person. With one respondent, about an hour was devoted for filling in the questionnaire as well as getting answers through a process of interview. Thus, no questionnaire was destroyed as incomplete. The schedule consisted of both structured and open-ended questions. Before finalising the schedule, we made a pilot study and pre-coded the responses that helped us in further improving the questionnaires for NGOs and citizens.

Data Analysis

After the completion of data collection, two elaborate computer programmes were prepared, one each for NGO and citizen respondents, and the data were fed into the programmes. The data were then tabulated with suitable 'find' commands and analysed. The findings were neither put to the test of statistical significance, nor were any correlations or coefficients found out, but only percentage distribution in interpreting the findings was deduced.

Bibliography

A Compendium of Partnership between Government and Voluntary Sector, Planning Commission, Government of India, 2002.

Abed, F.H., "Extension Services of NGOs: The Approach of BRAC" – paper to National Seminar on GO-NGO Collaboration in Agricultural Research and Extension, 4 August 1991, Dhaka.

Adams, W.M., *Green Development: Environment and Sustainability in the Third World,* London and New York: Routledge, 1990.

Adiseshaiah, Malcom S., "Testing Voluntary Agencies: No Good for This Big Task", *Yojana,* 28: 20 and 21 November, 1984.

Aguirre, F. and Namdar-Irani, M., "Complementarities and Tensions in NGO-State Relations in Agricultural Development: The Trajectory of Agraria (Chile)", *Agriculture Research and Extension Network Paper No. 32,* London: Overseas Development Institute, 1992.

Ali, Sofi, "Public Policy-Making in India: Lessons from Rural Development Programmes", *Indian Journal of Public Administration,* 38(2), 1992.

Allen, Tim and Thomas, Alan (Eds.), "Meanings and Views of Development" by Alan Thomas, *Poverty and Development into the 21st Century*, The Open University in Association with Oxford University Press, 2000.

Alliband, Terry, *Catalysts of Development: Voluntary Agencies in India,* W. Hartford CT: Kumarian Press, 1983.

Almond, Gabriel A. and Sidney Verba, *The Civic Culture: Political Attitudes and Democracy in Five Nations, an Analytic Study*, Boston: Little, Brown and Co. 1965.

Altekar, A.S., *State and Government in Ancient India*, 3rd edition, Delhi: Motilal Bangaswami, 1958.

Amanor, K., Wellard, K., and Denkabe, A., "Ghana: Country Overview" in K. Wellard, and J.G. Copestake (eds.), *NGOs and the State in Africa: Rethinking Roles in Sustainable Agricultural Development*, London: Routledge, 1993.

Amis, William D. and Samuel E. Stern, "A Critical Examination of Theory and Functions of Voluntary Associations", *Journal of Voluntary Action Research*, 3, 1980.

Annis, S., "Can Small-scale Development be a Large-scale Policy? The Case of Latin America", *World Development* 15, 1987.

Annis, S. and Hakim, P. (eds.), *Direct to the Poor: Grassroots Development in Latin America*, Boulder and London: Lynne Reinner, 1988.

Anwar, J. et al., "Towards People's Science Movement", *Economic and Political Weekly*, Vol. 34, No. 2, March 12, 1983.

Arbab, F., *Non-governmental Organizations: Report of a Learning Project*, Cali, Colombia: FUNDAEC, 1988.

Asian NGO Coalition for Agrarian Reform and Rural Development (ANGOC). "NGOs and International Development Cooperation", *Lok Niti* 5(4), 1988.

Association of Voluntary Agencies for Rural Development, *An Introduction to Some Voluntary Organizations and Rural Development Programmes*, AVARD, New Delhi, 1962.

Association of Voluntary Agencies of Rural Development, *Voluntary Action*, Vol. 25, No. 7, Feb. 1983.

Avina, Jeffrey, "The Evolutionary Life-cycles of Non-Governmental Development Organizations", *World Development*, 13(5), 1993.

Bartolomeo, J. Palisi, "A Critical Study of the Voluntary Association Concept", *Sociology and Social Research*, Vol. 52, No. 4, July 1968.

Bava, Noorjahan (ed.), *Non-Governmental Organisations in Development: Theory and Practice*, New Delhi: Kanishka Publishers and Distributors, 1997.

Baxi, Upendra, "Activism at Crossroads with Signposts", *Social Action,* 36:4 (October-December), 1986.

Bebbington, A.J., "Sharecropping Agricultural Development: The Potential for GSO-Government Co-operation", *Grassroots Development* 15(2). 1991.

Bebbington, A.J. and Farrington, J., "The Scope for NGO-government Interactions in Agricultural Technology Development: An International Overview", *Agriculture Research Extension Network Paper No. 33,* London: Overseas Development Institute, 1992.

Bebbington, A.J. and Farrington, J., "Governments, NGOs and Agricultural Development: Perspective on Changing Inter-Organizational Relationships", *Journal of Development Studies,* 29(2), 1993.

Bebbington, A.J. and Thiele, G., *NGOs and the State in Latin America: Rethinking Roles in Sustainable Agricultural Development,* London: Routledge, 1993.

Ben-Ner, A., Montias, J.M., and Neuberger, E., "Basic Issues in Organizations: A Comparative Perspective", *Journal of Comparative Economics*, Vol. 17, 1993.

Bennett, Jon, et al., *Meeting Needs: NGO Coordination in Practice,* London: Earthscan Publication Ltd., 1995.

Beveridge, S.W.H., *Voluntary Action: A Report on methods of Social Advances,* London, 1946.

Bharucha, B.H., "Future of Voluntary Social Work in India", *Indian Journal of Social Work,* March, 1961.

Bhat, K.V. and Satish, S., "NGO Links with the Karnataka State Watershed Development Cell: MYRADA and PIDOW Project", in J. Farrington and D. Lewis (eds.), *NGOs and the State in Asia: Rethinking Roles in Sustainable Agricultural Development,* London: Routledge, 1993.

Bhatnagar, Bhuvan and Aubrey Williams, *Participatory Development and the World Bank: Potential Directions for Change.* World Bank Discussion Paper No. 183. Washington: World Bank, 1992.

Bhatnagar, Bhuvan, *Non-Governmental Organizations and World Bank-Supported Projects in Asia: Lessons Learned,* Departmental

Papers Series No. 2. Washington: World Bank, Asia Technical Department, May 1991.

Bhatt, Anil, "Asian NGOs in Development: Their Role and Impact", in Noeleen Heyzer, James V. Riker and Antonio B. Quizon (eds.), *Government-NGO Relations in Asia: Prospects and Challenges for People-Centred Development,* Kuala Lumpur: Asian and Pacific Development Centre. 1985.

Bhattacharjee, Abhijit, "Voluntary Agencies: Identity Crisis", *Mainstream,* 27th July 1985.

Bhose, Joel S.G.R., *NGOs and Rural Development: Theory and Practice*, New Delhi: Concept Publishing Company, 2003.

Bilimoria, C.R., "Voluntary Social Work", in *History and Philosophy of Social Work,* A.R. Wadia, Bombay: Allied Publications Pvt. Ltd., 1968.

Biswal, Purusottam, *Rural Development through Nationalised Banks in Orissa with Special Reference to Cuttack District (1969-1984),* Thesis Submitted to Utkal University for Degree of Philosophy in Public Administration, Department of Political Science, Utkal University, Bhubaneswar, 1988.

Bobbio, N. *The Future of Democracy,* Cambridge: Polity Press, 1987.

Bornstein, David, *How to Change the World: Social Entrepreneurs and the Power of New Ideas,* Oxford University Press, 2003.

Boyer, David, *The Role of Northern NGOs in the Promotion of Sustainable Development in Africa.* Edinburgh: Centre of African Studies, 1990.

Bratton, Michael, "The Politics of NGO-Government Relations in Africa", *World Development* 17(4). 1989.

—, "Beyond the State: Civil and Associational Life in Africa", *World Politics,* 41(3) (April). 1989.

—, "Non-Governmental Organizations in Africa: Can They Influence Policy?" *Development and Change,* 21(1). 1990.

Brayne, F.L., *Better Villages*, Bombay: Oxford University Press, 1946.

Brodhead, T. and B. Herbert-Copley, *Bridges of Hope? Canadian Voluntary Agencies and the Third World,* Ottawa: North-South Institute, 1988.

Brown, David and David Korten, *Understanding Voluntary Organizations: Guidelines for Donors,* Working Paper 258. Washington: World Bank, Country Economics Department, September 1989.

Brown, L. David, "Organizational Barriers to NGO Strategic Action", *Lok Niti* 5(4), 1988.

—, "Policy Impacts on the NGO Sector", Mimeo paper for World Bank, EXTIE. Washington, D.C. 1990.

—, "Bridging Organizations and Sustainable Development", *Human Relations,* 44(8). 1991.

Cameron, C. and J. Cocking, *The Evaluation of NGO Activities, Organizations, Methodology and Results,* London: ODA, Evaluation Department, 1991.

CAPART (Council for Advancement of People's Action and Rural Technology). *Action Plan to Bring About A Collaborative Relationship Between VOs and Government.* New Delhi: Council for Advancement of People's Action and Rural Technology.

CAPART at a Glance, available at http://www.nic.in/capart/glance2.htm.

Carroll, T., Humphreys, D. and Scurrah, M., "Grassroots Support Organizations in Peru", *Development in Practice* (12). 1991.

Carroll, T., *Intermediary NGOs: The Supporting Link in Grassroots Development,* West Hartford CT: Kumarian Press. 1992.

Central Institute of Research and Training in Public Cooperation, A Study of Voluntary Services in India, New Delhi, 1969.

Cernea, Michael M., *Nongovernmental Organizations and Local Development,* Discussion Paper No. 40, Washington: World Bank, 1988.

Chadha, Prem, Jagadananda and Lal, Gayatri, *Organizational Behaviour: A Framework for Non-Government Development Organizations*, CYSD, 2003.

Chambers, R. and Jiggins, J., "Agricultural Research for Resource-Poor Farmers: A Parsimonious Paradigm", *Discussion Paper* No. 220, Brighton: Institute of Development Studies, 1986.

Chambers, R., *Rural Development: Putting the Last First,* Harlow: Longman, 1983.

Chambers, R., *Sustainable Livelihoods, Environment and Development: Putting Poor Rural People First,* Discussion Paper No. 240, Brighton: Institute of Development Studies. 1987.

Chambers, R., "Participatory Rural Appraisal (PRA): Analysis of Experience", *World Development,* 22(9). 1994.

Charyulu, U.V.N and others, "Integrated Rural Development through Voluntary Action", *Journal of Rural Development,* 4:1 (January 1985).

Charyulu, U.V.N., "Voluntary Organizations and Rural Development", *Kurukshetra,* (1st May 1980).

Chaturvedi, Anil, *District Administration: The Dynamics of Discord,* New Delhi: Sage Publications, 1988.

Chowdhary, D. Paul, "Field Counselling for Welfare Agencies", *Social Welfare,* 18:5 (August 1971).

Chowdhary, D. Paul, *Social Welfare Administration through Voluntary Agencies,* New Delhi: Atma Ram and Sons, 1962.

Clark, John, "Democratizing Development: NGOs and the State," *Development in Practice,* 2(3), 1992.

—, "The State, Popular Participation and the Voluntary Sector", in David Hulme and Michael Edwards (eds.), *NGOs, State and Donors: Too Close for Comfort?* New York: St. Martin's Press, 1997.

—, *Democratizing Development: The Role of Voluntary Organizations.* London: Earthscan, 1991.

—, *The State and the Voluntary Sector,* Human Resources and Operations Policy Working Paper No. 12. Washington: World Bank, October 1993.

Cromwell, E. and Wiggins, S., *Sowing Beyond the State: NGOs and Seed Supply in Developing Countries,* London: Overseas Development Institute, 1993.

Dag Hammarskjold Report on Development and International Cooperation, "Introduction – To Set in Motion the Process of Change", *Development Dialogue,* 1975.

Dale, Reidar, *Organisations and Development, Strategies, Structures and Processes,* New Delhi: Thousand Oaks, London: Sage Publications, 2000.

Dantwala, M.L., Harish Sethi and Pravin Visaria (eds.), *Social Change through Voluntary Action*, New Delhi: Sage Publications, 1998.

Dasgupta, Sugata, "Voluntary Organizations in Rural Development", *Voluntary Action,* 14:1 (January-February 1972).

—, *A Poet and a Plan in History of Rural Development in Modern India*, Vol. IV, Varanasi: Institute of Gandhian Studies, 1976.

Deshpande, V.D., "Code of Conduct for Rural Voluntary Agencies", *Economic and Political Weekly,* 21:30 (26th July 1986).

Deshpande, Vasant, "Developing Volunteerism", *Voluntary Action,* (January 1982).

"Development Alternatives: The Challenge for NGOs", Special Supplement of *World Development*, Volume 15, Autumn 1987.

Dharmarajan, Shivani, *NGO Development and Public Policy,* Delhi: Kanishka Publishers, 1998.

Dhillon, D.S. and Hansra, B.S., "On Making DWCRA Effective", *Kurukshetra,* September 1991.

Diaz-Albertini, Javier, *Development as Grassroots Empowerment: An Analytic Review of NGDO Programs in Lima, Peru,* New Haven CT: Program on Non-Profit Organizations, Institutions for Policy Studies, Yale University, 1990.

Dichter, Thomas W., "The Changing World of Northern NGOs: Problems, Paradoxes and Possibilities", in *Transnational Associations* 2, 1991.

Dichter, Thomas W., "Demystifying Policy Dialogue: How Private Voluntary Organizations Can Have an Impact on Host Country Policies", *Findings '86*. Norwalk CT: Technoserve. 1986.

Dick, H.W. and P.J. Rimmer, "Beyond the Formal/Informal Sector Dichotomy: Towards an Integrated Alternative", *Pacific Viewpoint,* 21(1). 1980.

Dube, S.C., *Indian Village*, London: Routledge and Kegan Paul Ltd., 1965.

Edwards, M. and Hulme, D. (eds.), *Making a Difference: NGOs and Development in a Changing World,* London: Earthscan Publications, 1992.

Edwards, M. "The Irrelevance of Development Studies", *Third World Quarterly* 11(1). 1989.

Edwards, M. and Hulme, D. (eds.), *Beyond the Magic Bullet: NGO Performance and Accountability in the Post-Cold War World*, West Hartford CT: Kumarian Press, 1996.

Edwards, M. and Hulme, D., "Scaling up NGO Impact on Development: Learning from Experience", *Development in Practice* 2 (2), 1992.

Edwards, M. and Hulme, D., "Too Close for Comfort? The Impact of Official Aid on Non-Governmental Organizations", *World Development*, 24(6) (June 1996).

Edwards, Michael and Alan Fowler (eds.), *The Earthscan Reader on NGO Management*, Earthscan Publications, 2002.

Edwards, Michael, *Civil Society*, Polity Press, 2004.

Edwards, Michael, *Strengthening Government Capacity for National Development and International Negotiation*, London: Save the Children Fund, 1991.

Ekins, P., *A New World Order. Grassroots Movements for Global Change*, London: Routledge, 1992.

Elliott, Charles, "Some Aspects of Relations between North and South in the NGO Sector". World Development 15(Supplement), 1987.

Esman, M.J. and Uphoff, N., *Local Organizations: Intermediaries in Rural Development*, Ithaca, New York: Cornell University Press. 1984.

Farrington, J. and Lewis, D. (eds.), *NGOs and the State in Asia: Rethinking Roles in Sustainable Agricultural Development*, London: Routledge, 1993.

Farrington, John and A. Bebbington, *Reluctant Partners? Nongovernmental Organizations, the State and Sustainable Agricultural Development*, London: Routledge, 1993.

Fernandes, Walter, *Voluntary Action and Government Control*, New Delhi: Indian Social Institute, 1986.

Fisher, Julie, *Nongovernments: Political Development of the Third World*, Kumarian Press, 1998.

Fisher-Peck, S., *The Road from Rio: Sustainable Development and the Non-Governmental Movement in the Third World*, New York: Praeger, 1993.

Food and Agriculture Organization, United Nations, Rome, *Study Guide on Development*, Freedom from Hunger Campaign/Action for Development.

Fowler, Alan, Organisational Vision, Mission, and Strategic Planning, (Paper presented during Development Management Course at PRIA), New Delhi, 1997.

Fowler, Alan, "NGOs as Agents of Democratization: An African Perspective". Mimeo (draft), University of Sussex, Institute of Development Studies, May 1992.

Fowler, Alan, "The Role of NGOs in Changing State-Society Relations", *Development Policy Review* 9(1), 1991.

Fowler, Alan, *Doing it Better? Where and How NGOs have a Comparative Advantage in Facilitating Development,* University of Reading: AERDD Bulletin 28, February. 1990.

Fowler, Alan, Nongovernmental Organizations in Africa: Achieving Comparative Advantage in Relief and Microdevelopment, IDS Discussion Paper No. 249, Brighton: Institute of Development Studies, 1988.

Fowler, Alan, *Striking a Balance: A Guide to Enhancing the Effectiveness of Non-Governmental Organisations in International Development*, London: Earthscan Publications Ltd., 1997.

Fox, J., "Democratic Rural Development: Leadership Accountability in Regional Peasant Organization", *Development and Change,* 23(2), 1992.

Frantz, Telmo Rudi, "The Role of NGOs in the Strengthening of Civil Society", *World Development,* 15 (Supplement), 1987.

Freire, P., *By Learning They Can Teach*, University of Dar Es Salam, Dar Es Salam, 1971.

Freire, P., *Conscientisation and Liberation,* Institute of Cultural Action, 1973.

Freire, Paulo, *Learning to Question: A Pedagogy of Liberation,* Trans Tony Coates, New York: Continuum, 1989.

Freire, Paulo, *Pedagogy of the Oppressed,* New York: Continuum, 1972.

Friedmann, J., *Empowerment: The Politics of Alternative Development,* Oxford: Blackwell, 1992.

Galnoor, Itzhak, "Social Information for What", *The Annals of the American Academy of Political and Social Science*, January 1971.

Gandhi, M.K. *Constructive Programme: Its Meaning and Place*, Ahmedabad: Navajivan Publishing House, 1984.

George, F., "Social Class and Organizational Dynamics: A Study of Voluntary Associations in a Colombian City", *Journal of Voluntary Action Research,* 1:3 (1972).

Ghosh, N.N., *Early History of India,* Allahabad: The Indian Press, 1964.

Gokhale, S.D., "Role and Responsibilities of International Agencies in Social Development", *International Social Work,* 1983.

Gordon-Drabek, Anne, "Development Alternatives: The Challenge for NGOs – An Overview of the Issues" in *World Development*, Vol. 15, Supplement, 1987.

Gore, M.S. and Khandekar, "Quarter Century of Social Welfare in India", in S.D. Gokhale (ed.), *Social Welfare Legend and Legacy,* Bombay: Popular Prakashan, 1974.

Gupta, Dipankar, "Civil Society in the Indian Context: Letting the State off the Hook", *Contemporary Sociology,* 1997.

Gupta, Ranjit, "Similar Concern but Varying Approaches: A Case Study of ASSEFA and MYRADA", in Dantwala, M.L. et al. (eds.), *Asian Seminar on Rural Development: The Indian Experience,* New Delhi: Oxford XIBH Publishing Company Pvt. Ltd., 1986.

Gurmeet, Hans, "Student Volunteers for Social Service", *The Indian Journal of Social Work,* Vol. LVI, No. 1, January, 1995.

Guru, D.D., "Role and Problems of Voluntary Health Organizations in Bihar", *Voluntary Action,* 16: (March-June 1974).

Guthrie, Robin, *Civic, Civil or Servile?* Geneva: Interphil, 1994.

Hadenuis, Axel and Frederik Uggla, "Making Civil Society Work, Promoting Democratic Development: What Can States and Donors Do?" *World Development,* 24(10), 1996.

Handy, Charles, *Understanding Voluntary Organizations,* London: Penguin Books, 1988.

Haq, Mahbub ul, "Employment and Income Distribution in the 1970s: A New Perspective", *Pakistan Economic and Social Review*, June-December, 1971.

Hashemi, S.M., "NGOs in Bangladesh: Development Alternative or Alternative Rhetoric?" Mimeo, Dhaka, 1989.

Hassanullah, M., "NGOs and Public Sector Agricultural Research and Extension in Bangladesh," paper presented at the Asia Regional Workshop on NGOs, Natural Resource Management and Links with the Public Sector, Hyderabad, India, 16-20 September 1991.

Hayter, Theresa, *The Creation of World Poverty,* London: Pluto Press, 1981.

Healey, J. and Robinson, M., *Democracy, Governance and Economic Policy: Sub-Saharan Africa in Comparative Perspective,* London: Overseas Development Institute, 1992.

Heaver, Richard, *Reaching People at the Periphery: Can the Bank's Population, Health and Nutrition Operations Do Better?* Washington: World Bank, April 1988.

Heginbotham, Stanley J., *Cultures in Conflict: The Four Faces of Indian Bureaucracy,* New York: Columbia University Press, 1975.

Hentschel, Jesko, Does Participation Cost the World Bank More? Emerging Evidence, paper presented at the World Bank Workshop on Participatory Development, May 1994.

Hewitt deAlcantara, C., *Modernizing Mexican Agriculture,* Geneva: United Nations Research Institute for Social Development, 1976.

Heyzer, Noeleen, Riker, James V. and Quizone, Antonio B. (Eds.), *Asian NGOs in Development: Their Role and Impact by Bhatt, Anil, Government NGO Relations in Asia: Prospects and Challenges for People Centred Development*, Kuala Lumpur, Asian and Pacific Development Centre, 1985.

Heyzer, Noeleen, "Toward New Government-NGO Relations for Sustainable and People-Centred Development", in Noeleen Heyzer et al., (eds.), *Government-NGO Relations in Asia: Prospects and Challenges for People-Centred Development,* Houndsmill, Basingstroke, Hampshire: MacMillan Press Ltd., 1995.

Hirschmann, A., *Getting Ahead Collectively: Grassroots Experiences in Latin America,* Oxford: Pergamon, 1984.

Holloway, Richard, "Doing Development – Government, NGOs and the Rural Poor in Asia", CUSO, 1987.

Hooda, I.S. (Ed.), "Rural Development: Some Conceptual Issues by I.S. Hooda", *Rural Development – Theory and Practice*, Rohtak: Spellbound Publications, 1997.

Hulme, David and Michael Edwards (eds.), *NGOs, States and Donors: Too Close for Comfort?* New York: St. Martin's Press, Scholarly and Reference Division, 1997.

Hulme, David and Michael Edwards (eds.), *Making a Difference? NGOs and Development in a Changing World*, London: Earthscan, 1992.

Huntington, Samuel, *Political Order in Changing Societies,* New Haven: Yale University Press, 1968.

Hursh-Cesar, Gerald et al., *Development Effectiveness of Private Voluntary Organizations*, Washington, 1986.

Hutchful, Eboe, "The Civil Society Debate in China", *International Journal,* 51(1). 1996.

Hyden, G., *No Shortcuts to Progress. African Development Management in Perspective,* Berkeley: University of California Press, 1983.

IRMA MDO Workshop Report – Workshop of Research Partners in a Nationwide Collaborative Research Programme Inquiring into "Management of Development Organizations", Institute of Rural Management Anand, May 1994.

Iyer, Paramesaran, "Creating Rural Employment: JRY's New Thrust Area", *Economic Political Weekly*, August 6, 1994.

Jagannadham, V., "Social Realities and Voluntary Agencies", *Voluntary Action,* 18 (July-August 1976).

Jain, S.C., "How Voluntary can Help Rural Development", *Kurukshetra,* (1st November 1981).

Jain, L.C., *Grass Without Roots: Rural Development Under Government Auspices,* New Delhi and Beverly Hills CA: Sage Publications, 1985.

Jain, R.B. (ed.), *NGOs in Development Perspective*, Delhi: Vivek Prakashan, 1995.

Jaix, Randhir B., "Role of Residents, Non-Governmental Organizations and Quasi-Public Agencies in Local Government in India", *Comparative Studies of Public Administration: The Role of*

Residents, Non-Governmental Organizations and Quasi-Public Agencies, Tokyo: Eropa Local Government Center, 1992.

James, A. Draper, "The Act of Volunteering: An Adult Educator's Perspective", *The Indian Journal of Social Work,* Vol. LVI, No. 1, January, 1995.

James, H. Copp, "Rural Sociology and Rural Development", *Rural Sociology,* 37, 4, December 1972.

Jayaswal, K.P., *Hindu Polity,* 3rd edition, Bangalore: Bangalore Printing and Publishing Co., 1955.

Kalimullah, Nazmul Ahsan, "The Political Environment of Non-Governmental Organisations in India: A Study of Three States", in Chaudhuri, Ranjit (ed.), *Conflict Development and NGOs,* Calcutta: Best Books, 1989.

Kannan, K.P. "Panchayat Raj Act: Local Self-Government and Decentralised Development", *Economic and Political Weekly,* December 4, 1993.

Kapoor, A.K. and Singh, Dharamvir, *Rural Development through NGOs,* Jaipur: Rawat Publications, 1997.

Karunakaran, K.C., "Voluntary Organizations and Rural Development", *Voluntary Action,* (January 1983).

Kavoori, J.C. et al., *History of Rural Development in Modern India,* Vol. I, New Delhi: Impex India, 1967.

Kean, R.C., *Anatomy of Disaster Relief,* London: Pinter, 1987.

Keane, John and Ian Shapiro (eds.), *Global Civil Society?* Cambridge University Press, 2003.

Khan, M., Lewis (eds.), *NGOs and the State in Asia: Rethinking Roles in Sustainable Agricultural Development,* London: Routledge.

Kleemeyer, C., "Cultural Energy and Grassroots Development", *Grassroots Development* 16(1), 1992.

—, "What is Grassroots Development?" *Grassroots Development* 15(1), 1991.

Korten, David C., *Getting to the 21st Century: Voluntary Action and the Global Agenda,* West Hartford, Connecticut: Kumarian Press, 1990.

—, "Micro-Policy Reform: The Role of Private Voluntary Development Agencies", in *NASPAA working Paper No. 12.* Washington

DC: National Association of Schools of Public Affairs and Administration, 1986.

—, "Third Generation NGO Strategies: A Key to People-Centered Development", *World Development,* 15 (Supplement), 1987.

Korten, David C. and Alfonso, Falipe B. (Eds.), "Structural Response to New Rural Development Strategies" by John C. Ickis, *Bureaucracy and the Poor: Closing the Gap*, West Hartford, Connecticut: Kumarian Press, 1993.

Korten, F. and Siy, R.F., *Transforming a Bureaucracy,* West Hartford, Connecticut: Kumarian Press, 1988.

Kulkarni, D.V., "Social Administration in Public Social Welfare Agencies", *Encyclopaedia of Social Work,* Vol. II, 1968.

Kulkarni, P.D., "Voluntary Action for Social Development", *The Indian Journal of Social Work,* Vol. 4, Jan. 1979.

Laclau, E., "New Social Movements and the Plurality of the Social", in D. Slater (ed.), *New Social Movements and the State in Latin America,* Amsterdam: CEDLA, 1985.

Lahiri, Aloka, "The Social Content of Panchasakha Movement", *Orissa Review,* Government of Orissa Press, April 2002.

Lakshman, T.K. et al., (Eds.), "Some Neglected Factors in Integrated Rural Development" by V.K.R.V. Rao, *Rural Development in India: A Multidimensional Analysis*, Bombay: Himalayan Publishing House, 1984.

Lalitha and Madhu Koli, *Status of Voluntary Efforts in Social Welfare,* National Institute of Public Co-operation and Child Development, New Delhi, 1982.

Lalitha, N.V., *Voluntary Work in India,* National Institute of Public Co-operation and Child Development, New Delhi, 1969.

Laufer, Leopold, *Israel and the Developing Countries: New Approaches to Cooperation,* New York: Twentieth Century Fund, 1967.

Lawani, B.T., *Non-Governmental Organisations in Development,* Jaipur: Rawat Publications, 1999.

Leach, Melissa, "Becoming a People Sector: Indian Voluntary Agencies at a Crossroads", *Community Development Journal,* 23(2), 1988.

Lele, Sharachchandra, "Godsend, Sleight of Hand, or Just Muddling Through: Joint Water and Forest Management in India", Overseas

Development Institute Natural Resources Perspectives no. 53, 2000. Available at http://www.oneworld.org/odi/nrp/53.html.

Lele, Uma, *The Design of Rural Development: Lessons from America*, Baltimore: John Hopkins, 1975.

Lewis, David and Tina, Wallace (eds.), *Development NGOs and the Challenge of Change: New Roles and Relevance,* Jaipur: Rawat Publications, 2003.

Lewis, David. *Management of Non-Governmental Development Organizations: An Introduction,* Routledge, 2001.

Lewis, J.P. (eds.), *Strengthening the Poor: What Have We Learned?* New Brunswick, NJ: Transaction Books, Overseas Development Council, 1988.

Litterer, J.A. (Ed.), *Organizations*, Vol. I, New York: John Wiley and Sons, Inc, 1969.

Livernash, Robort, "The Growing Influence of NGOs in the Developing World", *Environment,* 34(5), 1992.

Lovell, C., *Breaking the Cycle of Poverty: The BRAC Strategy,* West Hartford, Connecticut: Kumarian Press, 1992.

Maheswari, S.R., *Rural Development in India: A Public Policy Approach*, New Delhi: Sage Publications, 1985.

Malaviya, H.D., *Village Panchayats in India,* All India Congress Committee, New Delhi, 1970.

Manorama, B.H., "Women's Education: Role of Voluntary Agencies", *Social Welfare,* Vol. XI, No. 8, June 1965.

Masoni, Vittorio, "Non-governmental Organizations Role in Development", *Voluntary Action,* (March-April 1985).

Mathew, T. (Ed.), "Integrated Rural Development: Concept, Theoretical Base and Contradictions" by G. Parthasarathy, *Rural Development in India*, New Delhi: Agricol Publishing Academy, 1981.

Mathiot, Elizabeth Moen, *NGOs and Grassroots Development Work in South India,* Lanham MD: University Press of America Inc., 1998.

Mathivaanan, Dr. Samuel C., *Voluntary Agencies and Social Change*, Manas Publications, 1991.

Mathur, B.L., *Rural Development and Cooperation*, Jaipur: RBSA Publishers, 1996.

Mazumdar, R.C. and Pusalkar, A.D. (Eds.), *The Vedic Age*, London: Allen and Unwin, 1957.

Mehta, S.R., *Sociological Development in Mauritius: A Study of Rural Modernisation of an Island Community*, New Delhi: Wiley Eastern Ltd., 1983.

Mehta, Shiv R., *Rural Development Policies and Programmes: A Sociological Perspective*, New Delhi: Sage Publications, 1984.

Mendelson, Sarah Elizabeth and John K. Glenn, *The Power and Limits of NGOs,* Columbia University Press, 2002.

Meyer, Carrie A., *The Economics and Politics of NGOs in Latin America,* Praeger, 2000.

Misra, R.P. and Sundaram, K.V., *Multi-level Planning and Integrated Rural Development in India,* New Delhi: Heritage Publishers, 1980.

Mitra, S.K., "Rural Development: Need for Holistic Approach", *The Economic Times,* November 21, 1992.

Mitra, Subrata K., *Power, Protest and Participation: Local Elites and the Politics of Development in India,* London: Routledge, 1992.

Moen, Elizabeth, *Voluntary Sector Grass Roots Development in Tamil Nadu,* Tamil Nadu, India: Gandhigram Rural Institute, 1991.

Montgomery, J.D., *Bureaucrats and People: Grassroots Participation in Third World Development,* Baltimore and London: Johns Hopkins University Press, 1988.

Moore, David B. and Schmitz, Gerald J. (Eds.), *Debating Development Discourse (Institutional and Popular Perspectives)*, Macmillan Press Ltd., 1995.

Morgan, M., "Stretching the Development Dollar: The Potential for Scaling-up", *Grassroots Development* 14(1), 1990.

Moris, J., "Extension Alternatives in Tropical Agriculture", Occasional Paper No. 7, London: Overseas Development Institute, 1991.

Mouli, V. Chandra (Ed.), *Role of Voluntary Organisations in Rural Development*, Sterling Publishers Pvt. Ltd., 1990.

Mukherjee, B., *Community Development in India,* Orient Longmans, 1961.

Mukhopadhyay, K.K., "Volunteerism and Volunteers in Welfare and Development: Some Observations", *The Indian Journal of Social Work,* Vol. LVI, No. 1, January 1995.

Muzumdar, Kalindi S., "Voluntary Social Work: A Need for Introspection", *The Indian Journal of Social Work,* Vol. LVI, No.1, January 1995.

Najam, Adil, *Nongovernmental Organizations as Policy Entrepreneurs,* New Haven CT: Program on Non-Profit Organizations, Institution for Social and Policy Studies, Yale University, 1996.

Nanavathy, Meher and Kulkarni, P.D., *NGOs in the Changing Scenario*, Uppal Publishing House, 1998.

Narayana Reddy, G., "Human Resource Development for Voluntary Action", *Khadi Gramodyog,* 33:8 (May 1987).

Nelson, Paul J., *The World Bank and Non-Governmental Organizations: The Limits of Apolitical Development,* London: Macmillan Press Ltd., 1995.

Nerfin, Marc, "Neither Prince nor Merchant-Citizen: An Introduction to the Third System", *IFDA Dossier,* 56 (November/December), 1986.

NIPCCD, *Report of the Seminar on Role of Grants-in-aid in Voluntary Action,* New Delhi, 1981.

Non-Governmental Organisations and Micro-Entrepreneurship Development (Evolution and Strategies), Aseed, School of Entrepreneurship Management, 1992.

Orissa Reference Annual – 2003, Government of Orissa, Information and Public Relation Department, December 2003.

Pai, M.P., *The Emerging Role of the Collector,* Delhi: Indian Institute of Public Administration, 1980.

Pandey, K.C., *Rural Development in Modern India*, New Delhi: B.R. Publishing Corporation, 1986.

Patel, A.R., "Rural Development: A Challenging Task For Voluntary Agencies", *Kurukshetra*, Vol. 34(1), New Delhi, October, 1985.

Patrudu, B.V.S., "Voluntary Social Welfare Institutions", *Social Welfare,* Vol. XI, No. 12, March, 1965.

Paul, S. and Israel, A. (Eds.), "Non-governmental Organizations and the World Bank: An Overview", in *Non-Governmental Organisations and the World Bank: Cooperation for Development,* Washington, DC: World Bank. 1991.

Paul, Samuel, "Poverty Alleviation and Participation: The Case for Government-Grassroots Agency Collaboration", *Economic and Political Weekly,* 24(2), 1989.

Phadke, Sindhu, "Voluntary Resource Development: Content and Organizational Aspects", *The Indian Journal of Social Work,* Vol. LVI, No. 1, January, 1995.

Planning Commission, *Programme Evaluation Organization, Study of the Working of the Aided Voluntary Agencies in Social Welfare Programme,* New Delhi: The Commission, 1978.

Potter, David (Ed.), *NGOs and Environmental Policies: Asia and Africa,* Portland OR: Frank Cass, 1996.

Potter, David, *India's Political Administrators: From ICS to IAS*, New Delhi: Oxford University Press, 1996.

Potter, David, *NGOs and Forest Management in Karnataka,* GECOU Working Paper No. 3, Milton Keynes, UK: The Open University. 1995.

Poulton, Robin and Harris, Michael (Eds.), *Putting People First – Voluntary Organisations and Third World Development*, Macmillan, 1988.

Prasad, Kamta and Madaan, Davinder K. (Eds.), "Rural Development and the Role of NGOs in India" by P. Jagadish Gandhi *NGOs and Socio-Economic Development Opportunities*, New Delhi: Deep and Deep Publications Pvt. Ltd., 2001.

Rajshree Mahtani, "Enhancing the Role of Volunteers in Service Organizations: Some Managerial Issues", *The Indian Journal of Social Work,* Vol. LVI, No. 1, January 1995.

Randhawa, M.S., *Developing Village India*, Bombay: Orient Longman, 1951.

Ravindran Nair, G., "Welfare of the Handicapped: The Role of Voluntary Organizations", *Indian Journal of Public Administration,* 27 (July-September 1981).

Report of the Steering Committee on Voluntary Sector for the Tenth Five-Year Plan (2002-07), Planning Commission, Government of India.

Richard, Pine, "Community Development and Voluntary Association: Case Studies in Dinland, England and Ireland", *Leisure Studies,* Vol. 3, No. 1, Jan. 1984.

Riddel, Roger and Robinson, Mark, *Non-Governmental Organizations and Rural Poverty Alleviation,* Overseas Development Institute, London, Clarendon Press, Oxford, 1995.

Riker, James V. "Contending Perspectives for Interpreting Government-NGO Relations in South and Southeast Asia: Constraints, Challenges and the Search for Common Ground in Rural Development", in Noeleen Heyzer et al., *Government-NGO Relations in Asia: Prospects and Challenges for People-Centred Development,* Kuala Lumpur: Asian and Pacific Development Centre, 1995.

—, "From Cooptation to Cooperation and Collaboration in Government-NGO Relations: Toward an Enabling Policy Environment for People-Centred Development in Asia", in Noeleen Heyzer et al., *Government-NGO Relations in Asia: Prospects and Challenges for People-Centred Development,* Kuala Lumpur: Asian and Pacific Development Centre, 1995.

Riley, John M., *Stakeholders in Rural Development: Critical Collaboration in State-NGO Partnerships*, New Delhi, Thousand Oaks, London: Sage Publications, 2002.

Robinson, Mark A., "Assessing the Impact of NGO Rural Poverty Alleviation Programmes: Evidence from South India", *Journal of International Development,* 4(4), 1992.

—, *Evaluating the Impact of NGOs in Rural Poverty Alleviation: India Country Study,* ODI Working Paper No. 49. London: Overseas Development Institute, 1991.

Rondinelli, Dennis A., *Development Projects as Policy Experiments: An Adaptive Approach to Development Administration,* 2nd editon, London: Routledge.

Rostow, W.W., *The Stages of Economic Growth: A Non-Communist Manifesto,* London: Longman Inc., 1960.

Roy, Bunker, "NGOs Too Need a Code", *The Indian Express,* 29 December, 1993.

Roy, Bunker, "Open Letter to Home Minister: Foreign Funds and Threat to Voluntary Sector", *Economic and Political Weekly,* 7 December, 1996.

Roy, Bunker, "Threats to Volunteerism: Why a Code of Conduct of Necessary", *Indian Journal of Social Science,* 56(1), 1995.

Roy, Bunker, "Vanishing Voluntarism", *Himal: The South Asian Magazine,* 11(8). 1998.

Roy, Sanjit, "Government as Donor for Voluntary Action", *Voluntary Action,* Vol. 25, No. 6, Jan., 1983.

Rudolf, C.H., *Voluntary Action and Development,* New Delhi: Concept Publishing Company, 1988.

Sachidananda, "Voluntary Agencies and the Challenge of the Eighties", *Journal of Social and Economic Studies,* (September 1981).

Sarch, M.T. and Copestake, J., "The Gambia: Country Overview" in K. Wellard, and J.G. Copestake (Eds.), *NGOs and the State in Africa: Rethinking Roles in Sustainable Agricultural Development,* London: Routledge, 1993.

Satish, S. and Farrington, J., "A Research-Based NGO in India: The Bharatiya Agrol-Industries Foundation's Cross-bred Dairy Programme", *Agricultural Research and Extension Network Paper 18.* London: Overseas Development Institute, 1990.

Satish, S. and Kamal, P., "NGOs Links with Government Farm Science Centers (KVKs) – Seva Bharati: KVK", in J. Farrington and D. Lewis (Eds.), *NGOs and the State in Asia: Rethinking Roles in Sustainable Agricultural Development,* London: Routledge, 1993.

Satya Sundaram, I., *Rural Development*, Mumbai/New Delhi/Nagpur/ Bangalore: Himalaya Publishing House, 1997.

Seers, Dudley, "*The Meaning of Development*", Paper Presented at the Eleventh World Conference of the Society for International Development, New Delhi, 1969.

Seetharam, M., "Integrated Rural Development: Trends and Challenges", *Kurukshetra,* November, 1989.

Sethi, D.P., "The Voluntary Organizations in Social Welfare", *Social Welfare,* Vol. XI, No. 10, Jan., 1965.

Shah, Geeta and Revati Balu, "Short-Term Training Course in Social Work for Volunteers", *The Indian Journal of Social Work,* Vol. LVI, No. 1, January 1995.

Sharma, S.K. and Malhotra, S.L., *Integrated Rural Development: Approach, Strategy and Perspectives*, New Delhi: Abhinav Publications, 1977.

Siddiqui, S.Y., *Social Work and Social Action,* New Delhi: Human Publications, 1984.

Singh, Abha Lakshmi and Fazal, Shahab, *Agriculture and Rural Development*, Delhi: B.R. Publishing Corporation, 1998.

Singh, Katar, *Rural Development – Principles, Policies and Management*, New Delhi/Beverly Hills/Newbury Park/London: Sage Publications, 1986.

Singh, Kavaljit, "The Role of Voluntary Agencies in Economic Re-adjustment", *Indian Express,* 27th June, 1992.

Sitaramayya, Pattabhi, *The History of Indian National Congress (1985-1935),* Working Committee of the Congress, Allahabad, 1935.

Siviah, M., Rao, K.V.N., Murthy, L.S.N. and Mallikarjuniah, G., *Panchayati Raj: An Analytical Study,* National Institute of Rural Development, Hyderabad.

Smillie, I., *Mastering the Machine: Poverty, Aid and Technology,* London: IT Publications, 1991.

Stephen, T.S., *Guidelines for Voluntary Organisations*, PDC – Network, Bhubaneswar, 2003.

Swaminathan, P. and Satish, S., "NGO Links with Government Farm Science Centers – UPASI KVK", in J. Farrington and D. Lewis (Eds.), *NGOs and the State in Asia: Rethinking Role in Sustainable Agricultural Development,* London: Routledge, 1993.

Tandon, Rajesh, "Civil Society in India: An Exercise in Mapping", *Innovations in Civil Society*, Volume 1, No.1, July 2001.

Tandon, Rajesh, "The Relationship Between NGOs and Government", paper presented to the Conference on the Promotion of Autonomous Development, New Delhi: PRIA, 1987.

Tandon, Rajesh, "Board Games: Governance and Accountability in NGOs", in Michael Edwards, and David Hulme (Eds.), *Beyond the Magic Bullet: NGO Performance and Accountability in the Post-Cold War World,* West Hartford CT: Kumarian Press, 1996.

Tandon, Rajesh, "NGO Regulation: South Asian Scenario", *Transnational Associations,* 4, 1993.

Tandon, Rajesh, *NGO-Government Relations: A Source of Life or a Kiss of Death*, Society for Participatory Research in Asia, New Delhi.

Tendler, Judith, "Whatever Happened to Poverty Alleviation?" Report for the Mid-Decade Review of the Ford Foundation's

Program on Livelihood, Employment and Income Generation, reprinted in *World Development,* 17(1), 1987.

Tendler, Judith, Training Private Voluntary Organizations into Development Agencies: Questions for Evaluation, Program Evaluation Discussion Paper Number 12, Washington, DC: U.S. Agency for International Development, 1982.

Thapa, D., "United Mission to Nepal's Forestry Activities, with special reference to the Nepal Coppice Reforestation Programme", in J. Farrington and D. Lewis (Eds.), *NGOs and the State in Asia: Rethinking Roles in Sustainable Agricultural Development,* London: Routledge. 1993.

The Auroville Foundation Act, Delhi: Ministry of Law and Justice, Government of India, 1988.

The National Bank for Agriculture and Rural Development Act, 1981, (61 of 1981).

The Report of the Royal Commission on Agriculture in India, Government of India, 1928.

Thurow, Lester, *The Zero Sum Society: Distribution and the Possibilities for Economic Change,* New York: Basic Books, 1980.

Todaro, Michael P., *Economic Development in the Third World,* 3rd ed. New York: Longman Inc., 1985.

Turner, F.J., *Social Work Treatment,* London: Collier Macmillan Publisher, 1986.

Turner, Mark and David Hulme, 1997, *Government, Administration and Development: Making the State Work,* West Hartford CT: Kumarian Press.

UNDP Human Development Report 2003, Oxford: Oxford University Press.

Uphoff, Norman, *Local Institutional Development, An Analytical Sourcebook with Cases,* West Hartford, Connecticut: Kumarian Press, 1986.

Uphoff, Norman, "Grassroots Organizations and NGOs in Rural Development: Opportunities with Diminishing States and Expanding Markets", paper for the conference State, Market and Civil Institutions: New Theories, New Practices and their Implications for Rural Development, 13-14 December 1991. Published 1993, in *World Development* 21(4). 1993.

Uphoff, Norman, *Non-Governmental Organisations: Performance and Accountability: Beyond the Magic Bullet,* London: Earthscan Publication Ltd., 1995.

Vasimalai, M., "Professional Assistance for Development Action (PRADAN): An NGO de-mystifies and Scales Down Technology", in J. Farrignton and D. Lewis (Eds.), *NGOs and the State in Asia: Rethinking Roles in Sustainable Agricultural Development,* London: Routledge, 1993.

Voluntary Development Organizations in India – A Study of History, Roles and Future Challenges, Society for Participatory Research in Asia, New Delhi, November 1991.

William, R. Lassey, *Planning in Rural Environments,* New York: McGraw Hill, 1977.

Wilson, David C. and Butler, Richard J., "Voluntary Organizations in Action: Strategy in the Voluntary Sector", *Journal of Management Studies,* 23:5 (September 1986).

World Bank: The Assault on World Poverty, Baltimore: Johns Hopkins University Press, 1975.

World Bank Operational Directives, Washington, D.C.: The World Bank, 1989.

World Bank, *How the World Bank Works with Nongovernmental Organizations.* Washington, DC: World Bank. 1990.

World Bank, *Rural Development – Vision to Action, A Sector Strategy,* Washington, D.C., 1997.

World Bank, *The World Bank's Partnership with Nongovernmental Organisations (Participation and NGO Group – Poverty and Social Policy Department)*, The World Bank, May 1996.

Young, Dennis R., "Alternative Models of Government Nonprofit Sector Relations: Theoretical and International Perspectives", *Nonprofit and Voluntary Sector Quarterly,* Vol. 29, No. 1, A Publication of Arnova, Sage Publications, Inc, March 2000.

Index